R. D. Bartlett and Patricia Bartlett

Iguanas

Everything About Selection, Care, Nutrition, Diseases, Breeding, and Behavior

Filled with Full-color Photographs

Illustrations by Michele Earle-Bridges and David Wenzel

BARRON'S

2 CONTENTS

THE BASIC IGUANA

An in-depth look at the familiar green iguana may reveal what often transpires when one or more of these lizards are first encountered.

The Two Green Iguanas

The more widely distributed of the two species of iguana, the common or green iguana, is *Iguana iguana*. It is found in Latin America and occurs naturally on some of the Lesser Antilles islands. It has been successfully introduced in recent times onto other Antillean islands, Hawaii, and into extreme southern Florida. All these areas boast a subtropical or tropical climate, heavy rainfall, and lush foliage.

Iguana iguana has several very distinctive identifying characteristics. Below the tympanum (external eardrum) are from one to several grossly enlarged, rounded scales. Many green iguanas from Mexico and northern Central America bear pronounced hornlike nubbins on the snout. At one time, these lizards were classified as a separate subspecies, *I. i. rhinolopha*, but this designation has been declared invalid and those former members of the subspecies are lumped in with the common green iguanas.

I. delicatissima, the "other" green iguana, is properly called the Antillean iguana. It is rarely,

if ever, offered in the pet trade, and the only specimens I know of in the United States are in the Memphis Zoo. The Antillean iguanas lack the grossly enlarged jowl scales, and are found only on certain of the Lesser Antilles islands. Some populations of the Antillean iguana seem to be diminishing, especially on the islands where the green iguana is also found. Where the two share a range, the green iguana seems the dominant species.

Is an Iguana Right for You?

"Mom, *Mom!* Look! Look Mom! Look at this lizard! What is it, Mom?"

The answer, usually tendered with considerably less enthusiasm than the query, informs: "It's an iguana, Butch."

"What's an iguana, Mom? Look, Mom! It's eating lettuce. Can I have one, Mom?"

Now, with any prior enthusiasm altogether lacking, comes Mom's response:

"*No!* Absolutely *not*! What would you want one of *those* things for?"

Good question, Mom. Why indeed? And yet, when Mom and Butch leave the pet shop a baby green iguana goes with them.

An appealing, bright green baby iguana.

The Question of Survival

But what are the chances of this lizard surviving? How do you choose a healthy iguana? Once chosen, how do you care for it? From where did it originally come and how did it get here? How big does it get? Will it *really* survive on lettuce?

Unfortunately, the chances of most baby iguanas surviving for extended periods in captivity are not at all good. They get big—3 to 5 feet (91–152 cm) in length. Despite the fact that they are virtually always available in the pet trade, green iguanas have very specific care requirements. Furthermore, once an iguana's health has deteriorated to a point where its illness is observable, it is quite difficult to reverse the downhill slide that ultimately results in the death of the lizard. With this latter fact in mind, it then becomes obvious that you *must* keep your iguana in tip-top condition at all times.

Choosing a Pet Store

Purchase your iguana from a *reputable* and *knowledgeable* source. Unfortunately, many pet shop employees know precious little about reptilian husbandry. This is most easily reflected by the conditions in which they keep their lizards.
✔ Look at the caging. Is it clean?
✔ Is there a light above one corner of the cage to provide a "hot spot?"
✔ Is the drinking water fresh?
✔ Is there food in the cage, and what sort of food? Iceberg lettuce has about the same nutritional value for iguanas as newsprint. They need dark greens such as romaine, collard, mustard, and turnip greens, mixed with brightly colored vegetables and some fruits such as tomatoes and cantaloupe.

Find a pet shop with employees who can accurately answer your questions. To determine accuracy, compare some of their answers to your questions to the information contained in this book or in your other readings. They should jibe. If the pet shop employees cannot satisfactorily answer your questions, the chances are excellent that they are not caring for their iguanas properly. Shop elsewhere.

Choosing a Veterinarian

Find a veterinarian who is well versed in reptile husbandry. You will quite likely need him or her sooner or later (and unfortunately it will more often than not be sooner than later). The treatment of reptiles is a specialty practice. Not all veterinarians will be able to adequately diagnose and treat an ailing iguana. Ask your pet shop to recommend a veterinarian, or spend some time with a phone and a telephone directory and call veterinarians in your area. You might as well ask what an office call will cost, so you'll know ahead of time.

Considerations Before Acquisition

Prepare the caging for your iguana. The chances are excellent that you will be purchasing a (somewhat) stressed lizard. It must have a secure cage in which it can feel safe, with lighting and food in place (see pages 13–19).

The purchase of an iguana should not be done on impulse. You must also understand that iguanas have very specific needs for their survival. If you buy or are given an iguana, you are obligated to provide it with the habitat and food it needs. The entire procedure, from purchase to health care to feeding to caging, needs to be thought through. Properly kept, a green iguana will be 2 feet (61 cm) long at the end of the first year, and 3 feet (91 cm) long at the end of the second year. Its caging requirements will grow proportionately. Are you ready to share your quarters with a 5- or 6-foot (152–183-cm) long lizard? Of course, an iguana will not run up your phone bill or hide the remote to your TV. It will, however, require a changing and specialized diet, a sizable area to roam, and it must be kept warm.

Choosing a Healthy Iguana

How do you choose a healthy iguana? You let the iguana help you to do so. There are several criteria that you must consider. The initial health of your lizard may determine *all else* about its captive life.

Skin Color

Both the intensity of color and the very color itself, can aid you in choosing a healthy baby iguana. Baby green iguanas are green (rarely blue-green and even more rarely a grayish green), not a sickly, pasty green, but vibrant and intense—the color of the healthy leaves of a new growing plant. (It is the bright green color that draws most people to a display of baby iguanas, and interestingly enough, this same color permits the babies to blend imperceptibly with the foliage in their home country.) Unless the baby iguana is preparing to shed its skin—something that it does periodically throughout its life—a dull green color indicates poor health; a yellow-green often indicates impending death. However, vertical dark markings that may vary both in number and intensity are usually pre-

TIP

Baby Iguanas

For a very short period of time during the year, newly hatched baby iguanas are available to the pet trade. They may be either captive-hatched or imported. They are tiny animals, perhaps 7 to 12 inches (17.8–30.5 cm) in overall length, and still heavy with the egg yolk that sustained them through a prolonged incubation. Most have not yet fed; thus they have not yet been weakened by parasites. Should you be considering an iguana for a pet, these are, by far, the very best candidates!

sent. The markings near the shoulder and the hips are usually the most prominent.

Body Weight

Choose an iguana that has good body weight. Do not purchase one that has the bones, especially the pelvic girdle, starkly evident. As the health of an iguana deteriorates, the lizard will appear ever more bony and emaciated. A thin body and chubby legs is a bad combination (see page 41).

Demeanor

Choose a baby iguana that is alert and that has bright eyes that watch the movements around it—your movements, for example. And if among those alert, bright-eyed babies, there is one that is calm, or at least relatively so, choose it. The more nervous a baby iguana is, the harder it will be to tame it!

A healthy adult green iguana is an impressive sight.

When buying an iguana, selecting a healthy specimen is your prime concern. Learn to recognize the signs of good health as reflected by this green baby.

Young children and baby iguanas are a natural combination. Owning such a pet teaches responsibility and promotes an interest in natural history.

Baby green iguanas are easier to tame than adults.

Before buying an iguana of any age, locate a veterinarian near your home that is familiar with the needs of reptiles.

Checklist for Healthy Iguanas

	Good Signs	*Warning Signs*
Size	Newly hatched babies, 7 to 12 inches (17.8–30.5 cm) long are best.	Larger iguanas are hard to tame or handle; may not feed.
Color	Look for bright green coloration.	Yellowish color; mottled gray-green.
Demeanor	Alert and interested in surroundings but not frightened.	Apathetic attitude; closed eyes; "sleeping."
Behavior	Facing the front of the terrarium.	Avoiding front; hiding in corner.
	Actively sunning under heat lamp.	Not interested or too weak to move to heat lamp.
Appearance	No visible wounds or damage; no broken tail or limbs; no banged-up nose.	Wounds incurred in shipment will be slow to heal in a stressed lizard.
Feeding	Runs to food dish when it is placed in terrarium; begins to feed readily.	No interest in food.

If you can, watch the iguanas as food is placed in the cage. You want an iguana that approaches the food and begins chowing down. Admittedly, you may be in the pet shop after the iguanas have eaten their fill and are no longer interested in the food. But for obvious reasons, you want an iguana that recognizes food as something to be eaten.

Captive-bred vs. Wild-caught Iguanas

Generally speaking, support domestic herpetological efforts if at all possible. Buy iguanas that have been captive-bred and captive-hatched. Not only will this be an ecologically wise decision on your part, but there is a very practical reason

A wild-caught male green iguana responding to a perceived threat.

*Captive-bred tame iguanas of moderate size
will ride comfortably on a crooked arm.*

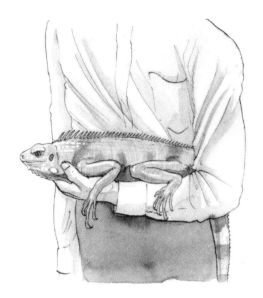

as well—your lizard will be healthier. A domesti-
cally bred and hatched lizard will be relatively
parasite-free or have a minimum parasite load.
Because food insects carry parasites, and iguanas
eat insects, the completely parasite-free iguana
may not exist. Captive-produced iguanas are
usually less stressed than wild-caught specimens,
and the balance between host and parasite is less
apt to become altered.

Warnings

✔ Never—not even for humanitarian reasons—
choose an iguana with dull, sunken eyes and
listless mien. It will probably not survive.

✔ Always choose an iguana from a clean cage
with ample fresh drinking water, a warmed and
well-illuminated basking area, *and* full-spectrum lighting (see page 18). The importance of
this latter item, although still being researched,
seems significant in inducing "natural" or "normal" behavior.

✔ As green iguanas grow, they lose the intensity
of color that typifies the healthy young. Adults
over 3 feet (91 cm) are predominantly grayish
green. They retain the dark markings of the juveniles. Occasional adults may be albino or brick
red; these are remarkably beautiful animals and
consequently are much in demand by hobbyists.

✔ Sadly, most subadult and adult iguanas are
even more difficult to acclimate than the

hatchlings. They are also correspondingly more
difficult to handle. Take particular care in
choosing one. As with a baby or juvenile, the
eyes of an adult should be neither sunken nor
dull and listless, nor should the lizard appear
thin and emaciated.

✔ Remember that wild adults can bite and
scratch savagely and slap resoundingly with
their tails. They have gotten to be adults by
fighting anything that looks like an enemy, and
you look pretty suspicious to them.

✔ Be sure you are able to handle and care for a
large iguana before the purchase. Most wild-
caught, imported iguanas will be very difficult to
tame, and therefore are dismal pet candidates.
They are also invariably heavily parasitized.

CAGING YOUR GREEN IGUANA

In the wild, individual iguanas wander over a large area. They climb agilely, swim adeptly, and spend considerable time on the ground as well. They move quickly from one area to another with no barricades. Theirs is truly a three-dimensional existence.

Caging and Iguana Behavior

Although it would be a virtual impossibility to offer the kind of varied and spacious quarters to a captive iguana that it has in the wild, large caging containing strategically placed "cage furniture," having a controlled, tropical temperature, and being illuminated by full-spectrum lighting is fairly easy to achieve. Proper caging is vital to your lizard's well-being.

You may wonder how an iguana can possibly get enough exercise within its cage. It would be difficult to build a cage that large, but there are options. Once your iguana is acclimated to you and to its cage, you may want to give it more room. If you have a room in which your iguana can safely wander, you could open the cage but retain the cage's "hot spot" for warming and the food and water dishes. Your iguana can then roam at will, returning to its cage for

A wire and wood cage on casters can be rolled outdoors.

food and water, and for basking. The disadvantage is that this will decrease the tameness of your lizard; it is the forced socialization with its owner that keeps the lizard tame.

Putting Iguanas Together

Although baby and subadult iguanas can be housed communally, adults are solitary lizards that stake out their territories and defend those territories vigorously against incursions by other iguanas.

Two maturing male iguanas that have been housed together since babyhood are very likely to become incompatible with age. Occasionally a male and a female will prove less antagonistic. If you decide you'd like more than one iguana, you need to be ready to provide separate housing.

Warning: Confine your iguana to a room or area that has no lamps to knock over or dislodge. Uncaged iguanas have started house fires this way.

Enclosures

Size

Enclosure size will, of course, depend on how big your iguana is and whether or not it is taken out for exercise or otherwise regularly handled.

For one or two hatchlings, or very young iguanas, a standard 29- or 30-gallon (109.8–113.6-L) aquarium will suffice. For one or two 18 to 30 inchers (45.7–76.2 cm), a 50-gallon (189.3-L) aquarium will provide satisfactory space.

Cage Top

Your cage top should be tight fitting and secured in a manner to prevent your iguana from pushing it upward and escaping. Even tame, relatively content iguanas will occasionally attempt escape. Commercially made terrarium tops that clamp tightly into place are now

available in most pet shops. If you choose to make your own wood-framed case, it is a small matter to hinge and secure a top. If the top is separate from the cage, use clamps or place a brick on top of each end to discourage unauthorized "wanderings." This may not be attractive, but it is functional.

You want to use either wood and wire or plastic and wire tops. This allows air circulation and permits ultraviolet (UV) rays from the full-spectrum bulbs to pass through and reach your lizards.

Larger Cages

As your iguana grows, it will require correspondingly more space, and the more space the cage will take in your home. A 3-foot (91-cm) long iguana will graduate to a custom-built cage that will quickly become the focal point of a room, if only by the space it requires.

Don't let the term "custom-made" scare you. Anyone with even a very moderate skill in carpentry can make a very suitable cage in an evening's time. If you know how to hammer, staple, and use a saw, you can make a cage.

Building Your Own Cage

Wooden framework and mesh: A simple cage begins with a wooden framework. Wire mesh is stapled to the outside of the framework. The bottom can be a piece of plywood—0.75 inch (19 mm) is best, but 0.5 inch (12.7 mm) will do—or can be wire mesh if the cage sits on a bed of newspaper. During the colder months, you may have to staple plastic to the outside to facilitate warming the cage.

Cardboard cartons can be used for hide boxes and when soiled, thrown away.

Caging of wood and wire construction may be made to fit an available niche.

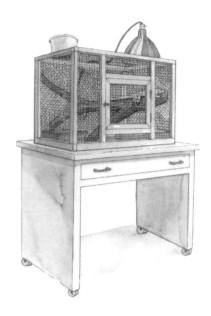

The supporting braces will need to be at least 2 × 2s or better, 2 × 4s, and the wire mesh 1 × 0.5 inch (25 × 12.5 mm). A smaller mesh is apt to catch the iguana's toenails and injure the toes. The mesh must be welded to prevent the lizard from abrading its nose if it tries to escape. The braces can be nailed or screwed together and the mesh stapled on with a heavy-duty staple gun. Be sure the door is large enough for you to reach to the bottom of the cage, to clean it, or add another door at the bottom of the cage for this purpose.

✔ For a 4-foot (122-cm) long adult iguana, a cage of 6-foot (183-cm) length by approximately 30-inch (76-cm) width by 6-foot (183-cm) height (just narrow and low enough to be moved through a doorway) will be necessary.

✔ If your cage is of wood and wire construction, build casters (wheels) into its construction.

✔ If your cage is of glass construction, sit it on a plywood platform that is on casters. The bigger the casters, the better.

Keep big cages moveable. It will benefit you, and your lizard, in the long run. If your iguana is out of its cage roaming about your room or home much of the time, a cage of somewhat lesser dimensions would be acceptable. In all cases, your lizard should be able to stretch out its full length to bask.

Lighting and Heat Sources

An iguana's lifestyle can be basically summed up in two words: "arboreal" and "heliothermic." These only sound complicated. Arboreal refers to trees, hence the climbing abilities of the iguanas. If there is a vertical surface, iguanas want to climb it, whether the surface is draperies, your pants leg, or a branch.

Heliothermic relates to the sun and temperature. Iguanas regulate their body temperatures by basking in the sunlight, more often than not while stretched out on a limb of a tree. If they're warm, they can digest their food.

You will need to duplicate a sunlit habitat within the iguana's cage. Iguanas like to sprawl while basking. They will position themselves lengthwise along a sturdy limb, drooping their legs and part of their tails over the sides. In the wild, such basking stations are often above waterways into which the iguana may drop if startled. Although you won't be able to provide the waterway, you can provide the "sun"-warmed limb. A limb with bark will be much easier for your lizard to climb and cling to than a peeled one.

A two-decker cage gives vertical room for climbing.

Many iguana owners end up building a large outdoor cage for their pets.

Although many of the smaller species of arboreal lizards do not hesitate to wander among the yielding twig tips, iguanas prefer the more substantial branches. Always provide your iguana with an elevated basking branch that is at least the diameter of its body, and preferably one and a half times the body diameter. The limb(s) must be securely affixed, to prevent toppling. Your iguana will feel secure on top of the limb.

Direct the warming beams of one (or if your iguana is large, two) floodlight bulb onto this perch from above. Be certain to position the bulb(s) so your iguana is unable to burn itself if it approaches the lamp. We have used large incandescent plant-growth bulbs for this purpose. However, a "full-spectrum" incandescent bulb has recently appeared on the market. This latter not only provides warmth but some of the full-spectrum lighting that seems so necessary to the well-being of heliothermic lizards. A temperature of 95 to 98°F (35–36.8°C) (measured on the top of the basking limb) should be created. You'll need to provide this sort of lighting-and-hot spot for eight hours daily; like any other creatures, iguanas like it dark at night.

This type of light and warmth is mandatory for the long-term well-being of your iguana. It is at a body temperature of 89 to 95°F (31.7–35°C) that your lizard is the most disease resistant.

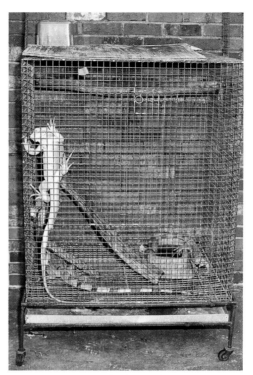

Left: Iguanas and other lizards use a shielded light to warm up.

Right: Even a fairly small iguana cage can be mounted on casters.

Hot rocks: We consider the "hot rocks" so often used with iguanas a very unnatural heat source for arboreal heliotherms. In nature, these lizards depend on alternating dark and light cycles to set their own body rhythms. They warm their bodies from the top down, by orienting and varying their body positions in relation to the warmth and position of the sun. Warming from the belly up is unnatural, and if your lizard happens to be gravid (pregnant), prolonged basking on an overwarmed hot rock *may* cause egg damage. You might consider this a minor detail, but we feel it is an important consideration and a valid concern.

Should you opt to use a hot rock, you must be careful that the surface of the rock does not get hot enough to burn your lizard. Remember: It will be lying right on top of the rock and its belly is less well protected than the back and side. You must also illuminate the surface of the rock. It is a combination of illumination *and* heat for which you are striving. Any heliothermic lizard—even one that is warmed—is distressed when brilliant illumination is not readily available.

CHECKLIST

Avoiding Electrical Accidents

It is important to use caution when handling electrical equipment and wiring, which are particularly hazardous when used in connection with water. Always observe the following safeguards carefully:

✔ Before using any of the electrical equipment described in this book, check to be sure that it carries the UL symbol.

✔ Keep all lamps away from water or spray.

✔ Before using any equipment in water, check the label to make sure it is suitable for underwater use.

✔ Disconnect the main electrical plug before you begin any work in a water terrarium or touch any equipment.

✔ Be sure that the electric current you use passes through a central fuse box or circuit-breaker system. Such a system should be installed only by a licensed electrician.

"Full-spectrum" lighting is available in both fluorescent (with UV emissions) and incandescent (lacking UV emissions) bulbs. The latter might better be termed "color corrected."

Full-Spectrum Lighting

In all truthfulness, the jury is *still* out on the role of full-spectrum lighting. Many iguana keepers, and especially iguana breeders, consider the use of full-spectrum lighting mandatory. However, others have kept and bred iguanas, and other heliothermic lizard species, without ever using full-spectrum lighting. We have never considered *not* using full-spectrum lighting.

Iguanas provided with full-spectrum lighting *seem* to display more normal behavior than those not so provided. And because normalcy is what you are striving for, we always suggest that full-spectrum fluorescent lighting be used in addition to the incandescent lighting already mentioned. To date, the hands-down favorite among the fluorescent full-spectrum bulbs is that known as Vita-lite. It is the UV-A and UV-B rays that you are striving to provide your lizard with. Even when new, the amount of these rays emitted by a bulb is low. To gain any advantage from the bulb, your lizard must be able to bask within 6 to 12 inches (15.2–30.5 cm) of it. Typical of any fluorescent tube, Vita-lite bulbs give off little heat, so the lizard will not be burned even if it basks virtually against the bulb. Position the fixture accordingly.

When I first began to use Vita-lites in the 1970s, my lizards reacted immediately. They were more alert and less tolerant of handling. These changes were consistent for types as varied as iguanas, geckos, and blue tongues. The new full-spectrum incandescent bulbs have proven equally as good.

Natural Sunlight

Natural, unfiltered sunlight unquestionably provides the best possible lighting (and heat) for your iguana. Earlier we stressed that your

A basking iguana is a perfect picture of contentment.

cages should always be able to pass through your doorways and be on casters. This will allow you to move your iguana—still securely caged—outdoors on warm, sunny days. In most cases the casters will allow a single person to accomplish this unwieldy task. Only cages constructed of wood and wire should be placed out in the sun. A glass terrarium filters out the UV rays and, even with a screen top, will intensify and hold heat. This can literally cook your iguana in just a few minutes, even on a relatively cool day!

Be sure to provide a shaded area for your lizard even in the wood and wire cages.

The advantage to having a cage that is easily moved outside is to get the UV rays. Window glass and Plexiglas will filter out UV rays while allowing heat through. Remember: If your iguana is basking in a screened window, when temperature allows it, open the window. If the window is closed, the glass will filter out the UV rays.

What to Do If Your Iguana Escapes

It happens so easily. You forget to latch the cage after cleaning it; you've just taken out the water dish and the telephone rings; you've opened the cage and remembered that you turned on the microwave with nothing in it. Whatever the reason, when you get back to the cage, there's no iguana inside. Where do you look? Are there places that iguanas always hide?

To a certain degree, yes. Iguanas look for places where they will feel secure—high up (on a curtain rod); where they are enclosed on three sides (on books on a bookshelf); under things (the sofa, for example, especially if the bottom muslin covering is torn and it can crawl inside); or behind things (a dresser or a bookcase). Check in corners and places where two or more surfaces come together to provide a secretive nook. Look under the beds, especially if they are covered with bedspreads that reach to the floor, and check behind the draperies.

The good news is that iguanas tend to forget that to hide completely, their tails also need to be out of sight. Look for a tell-tail, dangling from your curtains, hanging over the edge of a shelf, or extending out from behind the pots and pans in your cupboard.

Above: Some young iguanas have a blue tinge to their coloration, which may be natural or the result of diet.
Opposite: An energetic half-grown green iguana. Be sure you really want a pet iguana before purchasing one.

The use, size, and placement of basking limbs in the iguana enclosure have already been discussed. What more is necessary, to give the animal a feeling of security? Some keepers like to provide their iguana with a hide box, additional limbs, and greenery.

Greenery

Because iguanas are largely herbivorous they will not hesitate to chomp down on the leaves of living plants. It is imperative, then, that if live plants are used they be non-poisonous. Wandering Jew might be a good choice, although you will have to resign yourself to replacing the plant as it is sampled. It is also important that if you use greenhouse plants, no insecticides, neither contact nor systemic, nor spray-on fertilizers are present. The only fertilizer you can safely use is a concealed fertilizer, such as the fertilizer sticks you insert into the soil.

Plastic plants make a lot of sense. They can be washed, as they become soiled. They are generally sturdy enough to bear up under an iguana's weight, and you can simply staple the foliage where you want it. Iguanas generally test the edibility of the plants with their tongue, then lose interest.

A Hide Box

Even a simple cardboard box with an entrance hole will provide security for your iguana. You may want to use a hide box only on a limited basis. If your iguana can conceal itself every time you approach it, it may never become tame. While a hide box might be a good idea for a brand-new iguana, I would remove it after a period of two weeks or so.

The Flooring

The floor covering of your cage can consist of any number of items. Newspaper, wrapping paper, Astroturf, indoor-outdoor carpeting, cypress or aspen shavings (never cedar; it can be toxic to your lizard), or even rabbit food (compressed alfalfa pellets) are all ideal. The papers, shavings, and rabbit food can be discarded when soiled; the carpets can be washed when dirty, then dried and replaced.

Litter pan: Many iguana keepers have found that their iguanas will repeatedly defecate in a particular area of their cage. Some iguanas defecate in their water dishes (which must then be cleaned immediately), but others will quickly adopt a kitty litter pan containing a little sand. The cleaning of the pan is then a simple matter.

Fresh Water

A pan or tray of fresh drinking water should always be available to your iguana. Many iguanas enjoy soaking in tepid water as much as drinking it, and will spend

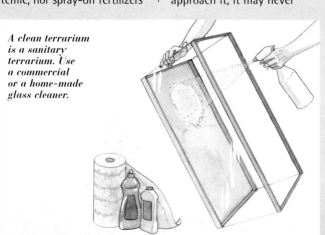

A clean terrarium is a sanitary terrarium. Use a commercial or a home-made glass cleaner.

considerable time in their water trays, size permitting.

Some iguanas do not like to drink from a pool of still water. Make a "drip bucket" by punching a small slit or hole with a pocketknife in the bottom of a quart-sized plastic bucket. Each morning, fill the bucket with water and place it on top of the cage where it can drip through the top screening into the water dish below. (Make sure the water dish is big enough to hold the water from the drip bucket, or you'll end up with a wet cage.) Empty and clean the water dish daily.

Misting Techniques

Some iguanas enjoy an occasional misting with a fine spray of tepid water. When you use a mister to offer water to your iguana, don't aim at the animal. Water squirted directly at an iguana may be interpreted by the lizard as a threat, and it could panic. Aim the mister upward so the mist falls like rain onto the iguana and its surroundings. You'll find your iguana perks up as the droplets descend, and if thirsty, will bend to lap droplets from its log.

Cleaning the Cage

In the wild, iguanas can move around and the buildup of debris is not a problem. Unfinished leaves wither and fall to the ground and decay, and partially eaten fruit is eaten by other animals. In captivity, conditions change. You'll need to clean your iguana's cage at least twice weekly, both to avoid any possibility of harming your animal(s) through the contamination of the food or housing, and also for your own sake. If the substrate is mulch, you can clean less frequently than if you use substrates of carpeting, Astroturf, or newspaper. Here's a fast way to stay on top of cage cleaning.

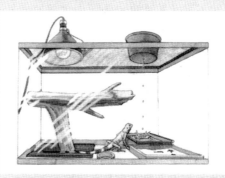

A drip-bucket may be necessary to induce a newly imported baby iguana to drink.

✔ Remove the iguana(s) and place it/them in another cage or in a clean trash can with a lid, so it/they can't jump out.
✔ Pick up the movable cage furniture and remove the flooring. If it's newspaper, throw it away. If the flooring is something more durable, such as Astroturf, shake it to remove debris. If the flooring is soiled, put it in your "to be washed" pile and find a fresh piece. If you use mulch, be sure to change it at least once a month or when dirty.
✔ If the enclosure is a glass terrarium, use a commercial glass cleaner to spray the cage, then wipe it out with paper towels. (You can make your own glass cleaner by putting a solution of 15 percent alcohol, 85 percent water, and two drops of dishwasher liquid in a spray bottle.)
✔ If the enclosure is wooden or wire, brush out the debris and use window cleaner on stubborn spots.
✔ Put fresh newspaper or new mulch down.
✔ Replace the cage furniture. Wash the water bowl, refill it, and put it in place. Replace the food dish, making sure the food is fresh. Put your iguana(s) back into the cage, and replace the lid and heat lamp.

UNDERSTANDING YOUR IGUANA

If you expect a pet that is as affectionate as a dog, or even as responsive as a cat, then you're better off with a dog or a cat, not an iguana.

What Do You Expect from Your Iguana?

Your pet iguana will, in all likelihood, recognize you as some sort of nonthreatening being as time goes on. It may even recognize you as a bringer of food, and approach you as you enter the room where it's kept in its cage. For instance, my iguanas look at me closely when I enter their cage; sometimes they'll come over to me. I noticed that they looked at me, then they checked out my hands. If I wasn't carrying food they liked, that "Welcome" shifted to a bored "Oh, it's you again," and they pointedly ignored me.

Handling and Petting

Many iguanas will become less skittish around humans, but steadfastly refuse to allow themselves to be picked up. I can hand-feed my iguanas, and they seem to enjoy the

Sheila Rodgers (Gulf Coast Reptiles) holds a six-foot-long male green iguana.

process, eagerly taking food from my fingers and checking out my hands for peanut butter sandwich "fingers." But there are barriers they prefer not to have crossed—they don't want to be petted or handled.

Some iguanas may allow some degree of petting but will respond to a human touch on the head or nape by biting or lashing with their tail. Both the head and the nape area are pretty much reserved for two kinds of holds—the male holds the female's nape in his mouth as he mounts her, and the head area is an area that no iguanas seem to ever enjoy having touched.

Way down on the list of mean-graduating-to-good iguanas are the few, the very few, that become completely docile and allow their keepers nearly any degree of liberty they choose to take.

It is for one of these few tame iguanas that virtually all iguana keepers are hoping. We can offer some tips on how to begin this taming process, but offer no guarantees that it will be 100 percent successful.

How Do You Handle an Iguana?

Suppose you've just been given an iguana, or your long-term pet is acting strange, and you'd like to examine its feet or otherwise check it over. Or perhaps you've taken your iguana to your veterinarian, and the two of you need to examine the animal. You can wrap it like a sausage in a blanket, but that's not going to enable you to look at its limbs, or position it for an X-ray. If you haven't tried this, you'll find your iguana can wriggle like a snake in its attempt to divest itself of your careful wrapping, and that its disposition will probably deteriorate in the process.

Martin P. C. Lawton, a veterinarian from Essex, England, recently described techniques he's developed for iguana restraint, neither of which require anesthesia.

✔ The easiest is to throw a towel over the head of the iguana. This reduces light and visual stimulation and the iguana will relax and become passive. With the head and body covered, you can gently move the iguana a limited degree and position its limbs. If the towel is dislodged, replace it and allow the iguana a few moments to become quiet again. (No one ever said that iguanas are smart, but you're not looking for a rocket scientist iguana here, just one that will hold still.)

✔ Dr. Lawton's "blinker" technique is named for the blinkers or blinders used on horse bridles to prevent them from seeing what's coming up alongside them. This technique uses a cotton ball over each closed eye of the iguana, held in place by an adhesive stretchy bandage wrapped around the head. This not only occludes the animal's vision and visual stimulation, but the gentle pressure on the eyes stimulates the vagal nerve, which in turn causes a slowdown in the heart rate and a drop in blood pressure. You have enough time to examine the iguana, or to position it for an X-ray, or to take blood for analysis.

How Do You Tame an Iguana?

Here are a few basics and a few comments that might help.

Keep in mind that an iguana's reluctance to becoming your friend is nothing personal, and has nothing to do with how you look or your socioeconomic status. By nature, iguanas are rather solitary creatures. They don't really like each other very much, except for certain brief personal encounters.

Dominance

For the males, the attitude to adopt is one of dominance. The alternative is to be dominated.

Being dominant is good. The dominant iguanas have the greatest success in breeding. The most dominant get the best perches and the most females (although I'll admit this isn't always as peachy as it sounds, as the females try to sneak out and mate with other male iguanas. Poor Mr. Dominant can hardly take his eyes off "his" females for a moment!)

To assert dominance, iguanas display against each other, bite each other, lash with their tail, and in a real "knock down, drag out" they may use their claws as well. Females are less dominant, but may develop at least some territorial tendencies.

In the wild, any creature approaching an iguana is either a female, another iguana, or may be a predator. If the approaching animal gets close enough to touch or grasp the iguana, survival instinct dictates that the touched or grasped iguana either flee or fight. It is this instinct that you (and the iguana) must overcome.

How Do You Overcome the Flee-or-Fight Instinct?

It may not be possible to do so, but you can at least try.

1. Until your iguana is completely used to its new home and to you, always move *very slowly*! An iguana will equate fast or sudden movements with danger more readily than it will slow movements.

2. You will soon learn what actions your iguana will readily tolerate and what it is more reluctant to allow. Concentrate on overcoming the negative responses. Again, always move *very slowly* when attempting to initiate trust.

3. If your iguana refuses to allow you to touch it, or to be held in your hand, try the same exercise with a thin stick wrapped with cloth at the tip. Some iguanas initially find this a more acceptable alternative than touching by hand. If your iguana will allow this, shorten the stick a little every three or four days until it is at last discarded and your hand is touching your iguana.

4. Remember that most iguanas will resist being grasped from above. If you wish to lift your iguana, coax it to step onto your hand or arm. Once it is clinging securely, restrain the iguana (if necessary) with your other hand and lift slowly. You will be able to move more quickly as your iguana becomes accustomed to this procedure.

5. When speaking to your iguana, use a calm, even tone of voice. You want your iguana to be relaxed as you approach it. Loud music or other noises may make your iguana nervous.

6. Iguana behavior changes after exposure to natural sunlight. The UV rays induce natural behavior, including aggression. If you have an outdoor enclosure for your iguana, or after you've wheeled its cage into the sunlight, expect your iguana to react quickly and unfavorably to any overtures you might make toward it. Many other lizards, such as the Gila monster, exhibit the same sort of wildness upon exposure to sunlight.

Mango Pieces

Whether the green is light or dark, uniform or barred, and whether the lizard is small or large, the normal color of green iguanas serves well to camouflage arboreal lizards when they are resting quietly on limbs in the dappled sunlight. At one hillside restaurant in Iquitos, Peru, diners vie to see how many iguanas they can see on the limbs that approach the open-air veranda. Over the years the iguanas in this colony have become used to the presence of people, and literally beg for the pieces of mango that the restaurateur keeps available, which are presented to them impaled on the sharpened end of a 12-foot-long (3.65-m) pole. The number of these lizards—some of which are 5-plus feet (1.5 m) in length—usually hovers at one or two (sometimes three or four) until the mango appears. Then the number, seemingly almost as magically as the lizards bestir themselves, doubles.

The Language of Color and Posture

The common name of "great green iguana" says it all. Or does it? During the breeding season, when adult males become suffused with orange, or even have the green largely lost and replaced by orange, the lizards may be green in name only. An adult male staking out or defending his territory can have all colors enhanced, and his alert posture will say, "I am the king." Out of the breeding season many adult male green iguanas are largely gray in overall color and laid back in demeanor. A warm, content iguana may be bright green, but that same lizard, if cold or upset, may be so dark that it approaches black in color. If it is ill, a green iguana often assumes a pasty yellow in color. And of course there is the new spate of colors—green iguanas that are never green. These are the albino and the melanistic strains that have recently become available.

Antillean greens: Females and babies of the increasingly uncommon Antillean green iguana are very green, but the grown males are duller. During the breeding season the face and jowls of sexually mature males become suffused with pink. Curiously, and for a reason (or reasons) not yet understood by us, when Antillean green iguanas are kept captive, their green fades to gray in only a few weeks. Of course, even when they are green, body language figures prominently in the intensity of the color.

Figian iguanas: The two Fijian iguanas have a ground color of bright to dull green. The females and juveniles are largely unpatterned, but the adult males are beautifully banded with robin's-egg blue to turquoise.

Spiny-tails: Adults of the various spiny-tails may vary normally from being largely of terra-cotta color, to turquoise, black, tan, or, during the breeding season, a quite brilliant yellow to orange. Males are often more brilliant than females. Darker banding is often visible, but

Albino iguanas have a loyal following among reptile enthusiasts.

During breeding season, the male's coloration may turn pinkish.

Left: The adult male extends his dewlap in his display pose.
Right: A young green iguana uses his tongue to locate a scent message.

for a short period after hatching, the babies of some of the larger forms are an intense green. They dull quickly with growth and by the time they are half-grown they are banded in gray or gray-black interspersed with dull green, or have assumed the darker livery of the adult of their species entirely.

Rock iguanas: The various rock iguanas are usually tan to black (babies are paler), and no odd color morphs are known.

Chuckwallas: The chuckwallas are tan to largely black (sometimes mottled), the latter with buff, yellow, or orange suffusions and highlights.

Desert iguanas: Desert iguanas are tan with maroon squiggles (no, that's *not* a scientific term) on their sides and back.

A young iguana explores his surroundings.

The Great Green Iguana

Since it is the great green iguana that is the most commonly seen of the iguanas in the pet trade, let's discuss its colors a little further.

The body color of the great green iguana, coupled with its body language, is a barometer of the lizard's feelings and health.

✔ If it is a male, the color and attitude of your green iguana will change more than if it is a female. Females tend to remain rather submissive and to retain their green coloration, although the latter may darken to gray-green, throughout their life. Whether or not the iguana is barred with dark pigment seems largely dependent on its geographic origin. Iguanas from some areas within the range of the species are barred; those from others are not.

✔ Baby iguanas should always be a vibrant green and alert. If they are dark they are stressed (cold or frightened); if of a yellowish tinge, usually associated with a lethargic, eyes-closed demeanor, they are ill.

✔ Except for being darker (for example, having a grayish suffusion on the scales), the color of an adult female is much like that of the hatchling. Darker than normal color equates with stress; pastier than normal color, coupled with impaired responses, indicates sickness.

Body Language and Color

Although they can vary dramatically by origin, adult male green iguanas have their own repertoire of color language, and a bevy of stances that are indicative of their prevailing attitude. Age—the male iguana's age that is—can change everything about a people-iguana relationship and, believe it or not, a 6-foot-long (183-cm) male green iguana in a "dominating or be dominated" frame of mind can instantaneously become a formidable adversary, especially toward human females.

Here are some examples of the meanings normally behind a male iguana's body language and color:

✔ Enhanced color or pattern: excitement, dominating territory

✔ Unusual orange or brighter than normal green color: advent of reproductive readiness

✔ Head-bobbing and dewlap distension: excitement, territoriality display

✔ Forelimbs straightened, eyes alert: alertness, a pose often assumed by a dominant male

✔ Head tilted to the side: alert interest

✔ Nose inclined upward, eyes partially to fully open: various meanings, among them contentment, basking, and alertness

✔ Nose inclined upward, eyes partially open to closed: contentment, basking

✔ Body raised high on all four legs, eyes widely opened, body not laterally compressed: alertness, but this is often not a dominating pose

✔ Body raised high on all four legs, eyes widely opened, body laterally compressed: a dominant posture, approach with care

✔ Body raised high on all four legs, eyes partially or fully closed: submission

✔ Inhaling and exhaling (hissing or puffing): dominance; an attack may be pending

✔ Making feinting motions toward you or actual attack (no this is *not* unusual!): dominance; be ready to defend yourself

✔ Dulling color: illness or the end of the breeding season

✔ Dark color: too cold

✔ Eyes closing as you near: submission

✔ Sprawled, legs splayed: submission, basking

✔ Whipping with the tail, elevating and compressing body: aggression; this may accelerate into actual attack, be ready.

Physical Attacks

Physical attacks by a pet lizard can be, at best, disconcerting for its owner, and can at worst, result in rather serious owner injury.

Always remember that even when raised as a pet, an iguana is a wild animal, the responses of which can instantaneously revert to single-minded, primeval aggression. Use care and good common sense at all times, especially during the breeding season. An admonition here, that you be prepared for what may occasionally be unavoidable, to be ready to get rid of a particularly unruly male, is needed. We recently had to face this. During one breeding season, our big, orange-hued, long-term captive male ("Simon Garfunkle" by name), became totally intractable. When we entered the cage to feed and care for the iguanas, Simon would bristle momentarily, and then leap in an effort to bite and whip us with his tail. To ensure our safety, we needed to carry a large, stiff, broom into the cage with us—our iguana cage measures $16 \times 10 \times 8$ feet $(4.8 \times 3 \times 2$ m)—and be ever-ready to fend off his aggressive acts. After many weeks of this, we determined it would be better to find a different home for Simon. We (and he) were lucky in finding Simon a zoo home, but this is not always easily accomplished.

Abnormal Colors

Now let's mention some of the abnormal colors—and let's add at the outset that many of these aberrant body colors don't change noticeably. Therefore, to determine your iguana's health and attitude, you must rely far more on body language.

Blue-colored great green iguanas have occasionally been found in the wild and have long been coveted by hobbyists. The blue may be caused by improper development of the yellow-producing xanthophores, but it has also been found that the administering of vitamin mineral supplements can turn a green iguana blue.

Albino green iguanas were once a great oddity and although they are now seen with more regularity, they are still not common. The babies are a chalky white with pinkish highlights. With growth and advancing age the ground color becomes more yellowish and the highlights are usually butter yellow. As with the albinos of many animals, impaired vision, often due to extreme light sensitivity, has been noted in albino green iguanas. More recently it has been learned that, when kept outdoors, in the course of normal basking, albino green iguanas will sunburn. This results in discolored patches and abnormal sloughing of the skin. It seems apparent that the care of albino iguanas needs to be monitored carefully on an individual basis.

Very dark iguanas: Quite recently a few very dark, but not fully melanistic iguanas have become available. On these, a suffusion of black pigment is very apparent on the back, sides, head, neck, and tail surface. The belly is nearly of normal green coloration. Although not particularly attractive, hypermelanistic iguanas will undoubtedly become important in breeding programs containing albino iguanas. The very dark example, when bred with the albino, then interbred again and again, should eventually produce a strain of pure white iguanas similar to the "snow" strains of many popular snakes.

DIETS

The health of your iguana, as with the health of any other animal, will depend largely (but not entirely) on its diet. Unless you feed your iguana the right foods–essentially a variety of leafy green vegetables–its health will inevitably decline.

Dietary Considerations for the Green Iguana

Because your iguana has been removed from the wild, it is subject to different health issues than those that would affect its brethren in the wild. It is highly unlikely that your iguana will develop botflies, be wounded by the talons of the predatory roadside hawk, be shot by a hunter, or fall from a tree and break its back. This doesn't mean there are no health issues—it is just that a large proportion of those you'll deal with will be dietary-based, as are a large percentage of your *own* health issues!

It can be difficult to tell what's going on with an iguana's health; compared to human medicine, iguana medicine is just beyond the discovery of asepsis. By the time the decline is tangible, unlike human medicine, where simple blood work can reveal a large number of problems, it may be too late to reverse it. Often problems manifest themselves internally, while your iguana maintains the "bloom of health" externally. It continues to eat, drink, bask, and

Offer fresh, bright-colored greens and watch your iguana eat!

otherwise respond "normally." Then one day you'll notice a swollen limb, or a slight yellowing of the previously bright green coloration, or a failure to respond as quickly as it once did to the presence of food, and the job of restoring health to your pet lizard has begun. The problem will be accentuated for, at times, a positive response by your iguana to a corrected regimen will seemingly be as slow as the decline.

A Proper Diet

Creating and offering a proper diet at the beginning of your relationship with your iguana is mandatory. In a way, it is even more important if you acquire an adult or subadult iguana than a hatchling. Hatchlings are nourished by yolk, and they're sent to wholesalers and the pet markets essentially once they crawl out of the egg. They haven't had time, comparatively speaking, to develop nutritional problems. They also haven't had the opportunity to develop a liking for foods that aren't good for them. If you offer a young iguana a good diet, one laden with fresh vegetables and a bit of fruit, both of you will be on the right track.

TIP

A Reptilian Cow!

If the dietary propensities of an iguana were to be compared with those of a mammal, an apt comparison species would be a cow. Like its bovine equivalent, the bacterial content of an iguana's gut will quickly and effectively break down and digest the high-cellulose content of leaves and other plant parts.

Baby Foods

For those specimens reluctant to feed, for ill iguanas, or for young iguanas, you can use prepared baby foods—without added salt or sugar; those with tapioca are fine—as a starter food. There is a wide variety of pureed fruits and vegetables available. Use an eyedropper to place a small amount well back in the mouth; pull gently on the dewlap to open the mouth. Be very careful not to place the food where it can be inhaled into the lungs, as this could cause an irreversible pneumonia. You can buy a stiff feeding tube at a veterinary supply house that will enable you to place the food beyond the opening to the trachea.

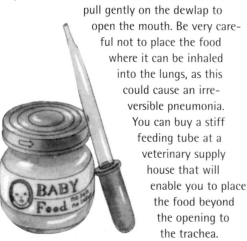

The Value of Iceberg Lettuce

Iguanas become habituated to the foods they are offered as young animals, whether or not the foods offered are healthful. Iceberg lettuce is one example. It has little nutritional value and a high phosphorous-to-calcium ratio, yet many iguana owners routinely offer it to their pets. Once acclimated to a diet of iceberg lettuce, the iguana tends to resist change. Whatever you offer doesn't look "right," doesn't taste right, and doesn't smell right. You can see the iguana looking at the dish and almost follow its thoughts: "This is food? I don't *think* so." After all, if you're used to eating pizza or sausage calzones for supper, followed up by a half-dozen garlic breadsticks, you may feel that tofu is not an adequate substitute.

Be patient and insistent. If iceberg lettuce was fed to your iguana before you got it, and it still insists upon it, use the lettuce as a tool, if you need to, mixing smaller and smaller quantities in with your pet's new diet. Vary the mix every few days—don't mix everything together in one huge salad. Use three types of greens one time, three veggies another, and other veggies the next.

The good news is that there are a large number of fresh and frozen vegetables to choose from. In some cases, the work is done for you: There are six types of bagged salad in my grocer's case; I find them handy for those days when I don't have time for (or feel like) selecting, washing, and chopping. I wash my hands and shake out the bagged salad for the igua-

Strained vegetable baby foods can be used in an emergency for baby iguanas reluctant to eat.

nas in the morning, and wash my hands again. In the evening I repeat the process, only this time the salad is for me.

About Diets in the Wild

For a few days after hatching, your iguana is nourished by the egg yolk in its body, but even within those few days, a hatchling iguana will begin sampling foods. Although even as a baby a green iguana is basically a folivore (leaf-eater), it may opportunistically sample an insect or some other form of animal matter. However, in the wild the base diet of an iguana, whether juvenile or adult, will be the foliage and fruits from the shrubs and trees that surround it. The young iguanas stay low in the understory and dine on shrubbery; adult iguanas are higher in trees and dine on the leaves there. The young iguanas typically consume leaves that bear feces from the adult iguanas, higher up. This inoculates the young iguanas with the beneficial gut flora found in adult iguanas.

Note: Hatchling iguanas kept isolated from this inoculation actually grow at a slower rate, because they are not as efficient cellulose "digesters" as their inoculated brethren.

About Diets in Captivity

We used to think that meat, in one form or another, was needed for the proper growth and nutrition of iguanas. We now know this is not true. Your iguana will get all the protein it needs from its vegetarian diet.

Not all of those fruits and vegetables that are of benefit in a human diet are similarly beneficial to your iguana. As a matter of fact,

Calcium, Phosphorus, Vitamin D$_3$, and Ultraviolet Lighting

Four important components in the well-being of your iguana are calcium, phosphorus, vitamin D$_3$, and illumination in the ultraviolet spectrum.

✔ Approximately twice as much calcium as phosphorus should be present in the diet of your iguana.

✔ Vitamin D$_3$ aids in the metabolizing of the calcium.

✔ Although the benefits of ultraviolet lighting are covered thoroughly in the "lighting section" (page 15), ultraviolet rays are so important to your lizard that we mention them again. Ultraviolet rays may be separated into two groups, UV-A and UV-B. UV-A induces normal activity patterns in reptiles. UV-B works to help your lizards to synthesize vitamin D$_3$.

✔ The UV spectrum of lighting may be supplied through the use of full-spectrum bulbs or natural sunlight. We strongly recommend the latter whenever and wherever possible; sunlight is free and unchanging, while the commercial UV bulbs have a limited distance effectiveness, about 15 inches (38 cm), and a limited effective life span of about six months.

some plants considered safe for human consumption, such as rhubarb, can actually be toxic to your iguana. Other plants and plant parts, while not actually toxic, can react adversely with other components of your iguana's diet and cause harm over a period of time. Spinach is one such plant; it binds up calcium and makes it unavailable to the lizard.

Top: A young iguana takes advantage of a dish garden planted just for him.

Middle: This baby green iguana samples a special commercial dry food. Such diets must be moistened before being fed.

Bottom: An assortment of suitable fruits and vegetables for an iguana diet.

What Should You Feed Your Iguana?

You can offer your iguanas natural, fresh foods, not necessarily organically grown, or you may want to use a prepared, commercial diet. Or you can offer both. Remove any uneaten food daily, and replace it with fresh food. Always have fresh, clean water in the water bowl. If you have no "feel" for the amount to offer, try putting in an amount that's two or three times the size of the iguana's head. Your iguana will eat more in warmer weather than in colder weather, and may eat little during the breeding season.

Fresh Foods

Vegetables: Speaking in generalities, vegetables are more nutritious than fruits, and for iguanas, the leafy vegetables are the most natural of all.

Choose from the following:
✔ Fresh or dried alfalfa hay—the dried alfalfa will need to be chopped—or the commercial rabbit or guinea pig pelleted alfalfa.
✔ Blackberries, strawberries, mulberries. Use both the fruits and the leaves; because of the high

An iguana in an outdoor enclosure feasting on a squash leaf.

A mix of fresh foods and a commercial diet is a good choice.

phosphorus-to-calcium ratio, the berries should be fed sparingly, but you can eat all *you* want.

✔ Broccoli stems and leaves are excellent. Florets have a high phosphorus-to-calcium ratio and should be fed sparingly, if at all. Your easiest route, if you like broccoli, is to buy the whole spears, either fresh or frozen. You get the flowerets; your iguanas get the stems.

✔ Cabbage. Remove the thick stems and chop for smaller iguanas.

✔ Cauliflower, all parts

✔ Cacti. The pads, flowers, and fruit of such types as opuntia or prickly pear are excellent foods. The spineless cultivars are the easiest with which to work; otherwise you end up burning off the spines or cutting them off, tedious work at best.

✔ Clover, fresh or dried; if from lawns be sure this is pesticide-free.

✔ Grasses, fresh or dried

✔ Greens

  – Beet greens

  – Carrot greens; the carrots themselves are too hard to eat unless shredded

  – Collard greens

  – Dandelion greens

  – Mustard greens

  – Turnip greens

✔ Kale. Remove tough stems.

✔ Legumes

  – Beans (yellow, green, soy, and other edible bean varieties); all plant parts.

  – Bean sprouts

  – Peas (including pods and leaves)

✔ Lettuce (romaine, leaf, or escarole), *not* iceberg

✔ Root crops (beets, carrots, parsnips, rutabaga, turnip); grated roots and leaves

✔ Squash (acorn, yellow, zucchini, etc.); all parts including blossoms. The fruits should be finely grated. Pumpkin, which is a giant squash, is among the least beneficial of the commonly available forms.

Fruits: Commonly available fruits such as apples, peaches, nectarines, plums, apricots, and most melons have limited food value to iguanas. Many are very high in phosphorus-to-calcium ratios, and therefore should be fed only sparingly. Although watermelon has only a fair food value, it does have a more acceptable calcium-to-phosphorus ratio.

Plants: Some commonly grown garden plants and/or "weeds" that are safe foods and usually eagerly accepted by iguanas are nasturtiums, hibiscus, and dandelions. All parts of these plants are acceptable food items. Rose petals are also eagerly consumed.

Breads: Breads should be just a small portion of the diet, no more than 20 percent by volume, but iguanas tend to like bread. Don't hesitate to experiment; I've tried my iguanas on a bread substitute, which was cooked rice stirred up with (unsalted) canned corn or peas. Pressed into a flat dish and cooled, it cuts fairly neatly into squares. My iguanas seemed to like it as a change. I've used peanut butter sandwiches, cut into easily consumed "fingers," as a way to add vitamins to a particular iguana's diet.

Prepared Foods

An ever-increasing number of prepackaged iguana diets are making their appearance in the pet market. Most of those that are readily available have been fully researched, and are rather complete in themselves. Some may be entirely so.

Although we would not hesitate to use the prepared diets as the main course, we would feel more confident if we augmented all with fresh vegetables and an occasional fruit.

Vitamin/Mineral Supplements

Even with a well-rounded diet, it is unquestionably best to occasionally enhance your iguana's diet with vitamin/mineral supplements. Those supplements most recommended supply calcium at a ratio of at least two to one over phosphorus. Vitamin D_3 is also an important additive.

Whether or not too high a level of vitamin A is detrimental to iguanas is not yet known. Since most fruits and vegetables are high in vitamin A content, supplementary amounts of vitamin A are probably unneeded.

Vitamin D_3 is *very* necessary to reptiles and amphibians. It aids in the metabolizing of calcium. While it can be synthesized in adequate amounts from an average diet if your specimen(s) have access to natural sunlight, inadequate levels of UV-B lighting will necessitate the addition of supplemental vitamin D_3. This holds true even with the much-lauded full-spectrum lighting. Although providing full-spectrum illumination is definitely better than not, the rays emitted by bulbs that are presently available are weak at best. The bulbs lose efficiency with age; although the light itself works, most of these bulbs emit a negligible amount of UV after six months—check the bulb package to find its effective life. For your iguana to get any benefit from the bulbs, they must be both new and positioned very close to the lizard.

A twice-a-week supplementing of the diet of healthy adult iguanas seems adequate. Rapidly growing baby iguanas should receive the vitamin/mineral supplements on a daily basis.

Iguanas with unlimited access to natural, unfiltered sunlight will require a lesser amount of vitamin/mineral additives than those having no, or less, access.

For more information on this subject see page 18.

Supplemental Calcium

Supplemental calcium is always recommended. Exactly how much is necessary remains speculative. Rapidly growing baby and immature iguanas most certainly have a higher calcium requirement than adults do. Specimens recovering from rickets or metabolic bone disease will need more calcium than healthy specimens.

Since ample phosphorus is almost always present in the normal diet of an iguana, many experienced and successful iguana keepers and

TIP

Some Vitamin/Mineral Supplements

✔ OSTEO-FORM (calcium and phosphorus with vitamins). This is a product of Vet-A-Mix, Inc. of Shenandoah, Iowa. It contains an excellent ratio of calcium to phosphorus, about twice as much of the former as the latter. It also contains a high amount of vitamin A (maybe not needed) and lesser amounts of vitamin D_3 and vitamin C.

Although this product contains more vitamin A than many herpetoculturists prefer, we have been very happy with the results produced by Osteo-Form.

✔ REP-CAL. This is 100 percent calcium and entirely devoid of phosphorus. It is a product of Rep-Cal Research Labs of Los Gatos, California. It also contains vitamin D_3.

breeders recommend the augmentation of the calcium alone. We have used both additives that supply only calcium and vitamin D_3 and additives containing a broader spectrum of ingredients. We can fault neither nor recommend one more strongly than the other. There are several excellent and commercially available calcium additives available from your pet store, your local feed store, your veterinarian, or on-line.

This chapter is by no means intended to be a complete coverage of all the diet-related problems that may befall your pet iguana, nor is it intended to supplant the diagnoses and treatments offered by your qualified reptile veterinarian. A qualified reptile veterinarian can be your best friend during times of trouble. His or her recommendations should be followed to the letter.

Diet-related Health Problems

There are several diet-related health problems that can be alleviated or avoided entirely by the correct diet. Think of these as the sort of problems (rickets, scurvy) humans used to have before the benefits of vitamins were known.

Four broad types of diet-related health problems are metabolic bone disease, gout, vitamin and mineral imbalance, and elimination problems such as constipation and diarrhea.

Metabolic Bone Disease (MBD)

In simplified terms, MBD is the removal of calcium from the bones to sustain normal calcium levels in the blood. It is caused by improper diet, although housing and vitamin balance play a role in this disease as well. The technical names for MBD are "nutritional sec-

Iguanas in the wild have their choice of foods—and their health shows it.

ondary hyperthyroidism" and "fibrous osteodystrophy." Common names include rickets and demineralization.

Symptoms: The symptoms are inactivity in your lizard and a thin appearance, except for its limbs, which seem plump. Sometimes the jawbone becomes foreshortened and the face looks chubby. These "plump" areas are your cue. They signal a major health problem, one where the calcium is leeched from the bones and bony tissue is replaced by fibrous tissue. Your animal needs immediate veterinary care.

Cause: MBD is most commonly seen in iguanas and other lizards that have been fed a diet heavy in phosphorus and light in calcium, such as iceberg lettuce, grapes, mealworms, spinach, and bananas. At first glance, the diet seems OK, but when you compare the phosphorus and calcium ratios, the diet is an iguana's worst dream come true.

To exist, an iguana needs a certain level of blood calcium. When the level drops below normal amounts, the parathyroid glands begin the complex process of drawing calcium from the bones to the blood. As the bones lose their rigidity, parts of the bones become overlaid with a fibrous tissue and the bones become malformed.

Prevention: The preventative agent for MBD is calcium. The causative agents are an improper ratio of phosphorus to the available calcium and a lack of vitamin D_3. Again, the calcium/phosphorus intake of both dietary items and additives needs to be carefully

monitored. The ratio of calcium should be maintained at no less than two to one over phosphorus.

Sufficient vitamin D_3 to enable your iguana to metabolize its calcium is also mandatory. Vitamin D_3 intake needs to be supplemented when your specimen(s) does not have access to direct, unfiltered sunlight. The natural sunlight induces normal D_3 synthesis, which, in turn, promotes calcium metabolization.

Even with a diet high in calcium, if the phosphorus ratio is elevated or D_3 is not present, MBD can and will occur. The debilitation is a long process through which your lizard will often continue eating and reacting "normally" until it is no longer able to do so.

Treatment: MBD is treatable in its early stages, and now, thanks to a procedure developed by Douglas Mader, D.V.M., a West Coast veterinarian, some (*not all*) late-stage cases may also be reversed.

The treatment for MBD begins with lab work to determine the actual blood calcium level. Once the diagnosis of MBD is confirmed, your veterinarian will begin three days of injections of calcium and perhaps of vitamin D. Following this period of stabilization, the synthetic hormone calcitonin-salmon is administered. This polypeptide hormone immediately begins to reverse bone resorption and to actually hasten the rebuilding of the bone structure. Because the levels of calcium and vitamin D have already been boosted beyond the ordinary day-to-day levels, the synthetic hormone can use them in the restoration process.

With this treatment, veterinarians are able to save the lives of many reptiles with MBD, but the honest truth is that such treatment isn't necessary, if your iguana has the correct diet.

Gout

If insufficiently hydrated, an iguana may develop gout. It is caused by a buildup of urates in and around the joints. Folivorous and herbivorous reptiles are especially susceptible to this painful condition if adequate, clean drinking water is not continually present. Iguanas are not overly bright and your lizard may not recognize its drinking water. The dish should be large enough for your lizard to soak in, and you may actually need to place your iguana in the dish before it recognizes it. (Of course, the cage's "hot spot" will be warm enough to dry and warm the lizard when it leaves its water dish.) Use the drip bucket method to create motion at the surface of the water in the dish (see page 23). Offer some water with an eyedropper. Spray the plants in the enclosure with water, so your iguana can swallow the droplets. Proper hydration and a diet with the right calcium phosphorus balance almost always ensures proper elimination of the causative urates.

Vitamin/Mineral Imbalances

Throughout this text, the importance of vitamins and minerals in correct proportions has been stressed (see page 38); this aspect is *very* important.

Iguanas will imprint on many foodstuffs and devour even those with little nutritional value with gusto. To all iguana diets it will be necessary to add at least two components, calcium and vitamin D_3.

✔ Calcium is necessary for proper bone development and life itself. Ultraviolet rays allow reptiles to properly metabolize calcium. A

Swollen limbs generally indicate metabolic bone disease, a problem which requires veterinary care.

pinch, sprinkled over the food twice a week, is adequate.

✔ Vitamin D_3 is necessary to help a reptile synthesize the calcium. Again, keep the amount administered small; too much D_3 will allow too much calcium to be absorbed.

✔ Phosphorus, present in most foods, can hinder the proper metabolizing of calcium.

✔ Vitamin A is usually present in adequate amounts in the diet of your iguana. Vitamin A enhancement is seldom necessary.

✔ Vitamin B. Of the various B vitamins, it is only B_1 (thiamin) that may prove a problem to your iguana, and this only if the lizard is allowed to consume plant life containing the enzyme thiaminase. Thiaminase, contained in many commonly grown houseplants, can inhibit the metabolization of vitamin B_1. The B complex vitamins can also be destroyed by medications. If it has been necessary to treat your iguana with antibiotics, the B complex vitamins should be replenished to assure proper digestion.

✔ Vitamin C is adequately present in balanced diets. A deficiency would manifest itself in hemorrhaging of the mucous membranes and bruising, which appear as dark marks in iguanas.

✔ Vitamin D. The integral role of vitamin D_3 in the health of your iguana has already been discussed in detail (see page 38). The other D complex vitamins seem somewhat less important and are usually re-sent in sufficient amounts.

Expelling Salt

By sneezing, iguanas expel salts that have been concentrated by salt-removal glands in their nasal cavities. This is an entirely normal method of salt removal. The expelling of these salts, often noticed first by the keeper as crystals around the nostrils of the iguana or as crystals on the glass of the terrarium, is not a cause for alarm.

Stressed by handling, young iguanas will often darken in color.

✔ Vitamin E deficiencies are diet-related. Feeding your iguana as the herbivore it is will assure that no E-vitamin deficiencies occur.

Constipation and Diarrhea

The normal bowel movements of iguanas vary remarkably in consistency. Those of a properly hydrated lizard will be well formed but moist. Those of dehydrating specimens will be dry.

Bowel movements do *not* necessarily occur at regular intervals. The body temperature of your lizard will largely determine the speed with which digestions occur. Cooler lizards will stool less frequently than specimens kept at warmer temperatures.

Causes of Constipation

If an iguana is kept too cool, the digestion process may either stop entirely or be so inhibited that ingested foods spoil in the stomach. In extreme cases the lizard may vomit these masses. Properly warm temperatures are mandatory for normal digestive processes to occur. An ideal daytime temperature range would be between 86 and 94°F (30–34.4°C). Slightly cooler—77 to 80°F (25–26.7°C)— nighttime temperatures are permissible.

Impactions: The failure of an iguana to stool may also result from a gastrointestinal impaction. Impactions may be caused by ingested stones, kitty litter, or other such materials, as well as abnormally dry stools in underhydrated iguanas. The problem is generally diagnosed by X ray. Again, proper hydration will preclude many problems.

A period of activity, such as swimming in a tub of tepid water, may induce stooling. However, large, immovable impactions may require veterinary intervention. Some impactions may

Iguanas are packaged in fabric bags, then packed in Styrofoam boxes within wooden boxes, before being shipped.

respond to small amounts of softening agents or lubricants available from your pharmacy. Use small amounts of petroleum jelly, milk of magnesia, or Siblin administered orally.

Fecal material that is not expelled has more and more moisture removed from it the longer it stays in the iguana's body, then normal bowel peristaltic motion cannot expel it. These stubborn impactions may require surgical removal.

Causes of Diarrhea

Diarrhea or abnormally loose stools can be caused by a diet change, by feeding too much fruit, by periods of stress, during illness, or other such anomalies. In most cases, this is nothing to worry about. Cutting back on fruit and/or adding items with a higher fiber content will likely correct the problem. Make sure that adequate clean drinking water is readily available.

If the condition doesn't clear up within a day or two, the problem may be caused by an internal parasite or a bacterial or viral infection, and you'll need to take your iguana to your veterinarian. Remember that not all intestinal "parasites" are actually parasites; it now seems that trematodes in the gut may assist in digestion.

Pathogens and Parasites

Respiratory Ailments

One morning you walk over to your new iguana's cage, carrying a bowl of freshly prepared calcium- and phosphorus-balanced food, and you look at your iguana. Something is wrong. Instead of scurrying over to the cage door, ready to leap on top of its food bowl, your iguana is under its hot spot, head down, nose running. It isn't interested in food. What has happened? What can you do?

Well-acclimated, properly maintained iguanas are not prone to respiratory ailments. But stressed new imports and marginally healthy iguanas, as well as those subjected to unnatural periods of cold—especially *humid* cold—may occasionally come down with colds or pneumonia. Some respiratory ailments may also be associated with the weakening brought about by an untenably heavy endoparasite burden.

Stress, then, of one kind or another, is usually the culprit to which the origin of a respiratory ailment can be traced. How many times have you seen someone go through a very stressful time, only to have the burden of a bad cold added to the problems? It happens to iguanas, too.

Respiratory ailments are initially accompanied by sneezing, lethargic demeanor and unnaturally rapid, often shallow, breathing. As the ailment worsens, rasping and bubbling may accompany each of your iguana's breaths. At this stage it is often critical and can be fatal.

CHECKLIST

Respiratory Problems

1. Cage your iguana properly; prevent stress!
2. If kept with a cagemate—iguana or otherwise—be certain all are compatible.
3. Have your iguana checked for parasites.
4. Keep temperatures within norms at all times.
5. In northern climes have backup heating systems in place.
6. Feed your iguana a proper diet

Treatment

✔ The first thing to do is to warm up the basking area. It is essential to elevate the temperature of your iguana's basking area to 96 to 98°F (35.6–36.7°C). The ambient cage temperature should be 88 to 92°F (31–33.3°C).

✔ Set your backup heating system on a thermostat, with the target temperature set below the ambient cage temperature.

✔ Be sure to offer extra food; many iguanas cannot fight off a respiratory ailment because they don't have any extra energy to do so.

✔ If the symptoms of respiratory distress do not ameliorate within a day or two, antibiotic treatment will be necessary.

There are many "safe" drugs available, but some respiratory problems do not respond well to these. The newer aminoglycoside drugs are more effective, but correspondingly more dangerous. There is little latitude in dosage amounts and the iguana *must* be well hydrated to ensure against renal (kidney) damage. The injection site for aminoglycosides must be *anterior* to mid-body to assure that the renal-portal system is not affected. It is mandatory that your veterinarian be well acquainted with reptilian medicine to assure that the correct decisions are made.

Medical Treatment for Parasitism

Many iguanas, even those that are captive-bred and captive-hatched, may harbor internal parasites. Because of the complexities of identification of endoparasites, and the necessity to accurately weigh specimens to be treated as well as to measure dosages, the eradication—or control—of internal parasites is best left to your veterinarian.

Endoparasites

The presence of internal parasites in wild-caught iguanas is a foregone conclusion. Recent studies have indicated that blanket treatment of all wild-caught iguanas may not be necessary or advisable. We feel that discrimination should be used by the veterinarian in determining whether or not to treat the specimen in question. Endoparasitic loads can actually diminish if you keep the cage of your specimen scrupulously clean, thereby preventing reinfestation.

Ectoparasites

External parasites are less problematic to treat than endoparasites. Only two kinds, ticks and mites, are seen with any degree of regularity. Both ticks and mites feed on the body fluids of their hosts. Both are easily overlooked.

Ticks are the larger of the two, deflated and seedlike when empty, rounded and bladderlike when engorged. It is best if they are removed singly whenever seen. They imbed their mouthparts deeply when feeding, and if merely pulled from the lizard, these may break off in the wound. It is best to first dust them individually with Sevin powder or to rub their body parts with rubbing alcohol, then return a few minutes later and pull the ticks gently off with a pair of tweezers.

Thanks to the advent of No-Pest Strips (2.2 dichlorovinyl dimethyl phosphate), mites are easily managed. A small square—approximately 3/4 × 3/4 inches (19 × 19 mm)—placed in the iguana tank, but out of reach of the lizard, for from 12 to 24 hours will usually kill all adult mites. If some survive the initial treatment, treat again a day later. No-Pest Strips do not destroy mite eggs; therefore, it will be necessary to repeat the entire treatment nine days later.

Other Diseases and Maladies

Several other diseases and maladies may more rarely befall your pet iguana. Among these are:

Mineralization of internal organs: This is caused by overmetabolism of calcium. Known as hypercalcemia, a treatment has been developed. It is both lengthy and expensive, requiring about two weeks of monitoring by a veterinarian. There is a fine line between enough and too much calcium and vitamin D_3. Once diagnosed and treated, you'll need to monitor and control your lizard's calcium and D_3 intake. If untreated or too far advanced this can be a fatal problem.

Diabetes: This disease is caused by pancreatic dysfunction. As in diabetic humans, a program of regular and continuing insulin injections can be undertaken. The alternative is euthanasia.

Herpes virus: This is a pathogen for green iguanas. There is no treatment. When diagnosed, euthanasia of the lizard is recommended.

Injuries

Despite the best care you can give, sometimes iguanas are injured: They find a way to lodge themselves between a heating lamp and the enclosure and get burned; a staple in a cage may break off and the jagged edge may tear an iguana's skin; the lizard may be injured in the shipping process en route to the pet store. With animals, as with small children, you can adopt a corollary of Murphy's Law: They can get hurt in ways you least expect.

Burns

Your captive iguana can be burned in any of several ways. The most frequent of these involves your lizard being in prolonged contact with a cage heating or lighting element that is either malfunctioning or for which proper protection has not been installed. Iguanas are not smart enough to move away from a bulb or a hot rock that is too hot; these heat sources don't occur in the wild, and your iguana has no knowledge of the danger they can pose. Among others, hot rocks, other heating units, and incandescent light bulbs have been implicated in superficial to severe burning incidents.

Burned areas are often discolored but usually not blistered. Treatment will depend upon the severity of the burn. Superficial burns will often require no treatment at all, but the causative agent must, of course, be modified, buffered, or removed. Moderate burns will

This iguana was allowed to get too close to a heat source, and burns are the result.

Heat and other incandescent bulbs will need to be carefully placed, too. Burns from a high wattage, heat-emitting bulb are even more possible than from hot rocks.

Cuts and Abrasions

Cuts and abrasions may be as diverse as burns in severity. If the wound is dirty, you'll need to wash it with soap and water, and rinse well. For the most minimal of these problems an over-the-counter antiseptic ointment will suffice. If possible, the area should be protected from dirt until it heals. The problem is that commercial adhesive bandages won't stick to iguana skin. Many hobbyists have found that one or two light applications of a liquid bandage such as Liquidskin seals the area with a clear coating. Be warned: Most of these liquid bandages contain alcohol and sting when sprayed on. For the more serious, veterinary assistance should be immediately sought.

Nose Rubbing

One of the most common causes of abrasion is also one of the most difficult to correct: nose rubbing.

Nose rubbing by tame iguanas that are used to "the run of the house" is self-explanatory. Nose rubbing by fearful wild iguanas that are trying unsuccessfully to return to the wild is equally easily explained.

Three ways of lessening the problem include providing a larger cage, providing a greater feeling of security, and more actual "freedom." Often, covering at least three sides of the cage

need to be cleaned and antiseptic ointment applied, especially if there are suppurations. Severe burns will need vigorous medical treatment and your veterinarian should be consulted immediately.

Heating devices: As previously mentioned, we are not proponents of hot rocks or heat bricks or other similar belly-oriented heating devices. Iguanas (and other basking species) are usually heliothermic animals. They thermoregulate by basking in the sunlight until warm, then move to a more shaded area so as not to overheat. This should not be construed as meaning that on cloudy days, or even at other times when they are cool, they will not happily rest on a warmed surface. They will! It is just that they are not usually forced to do so on a regular basis. It is much more natural if your lizard is heated from above, and apparently the lizards feel the same way. Iguanas (and other heliotherms) will usually more readily and regularly utilize a lighted area warmed by a heat bulb than the nonilluminated, ventrally oriented hot rocks with which they are so often supplied.

Shedding is a normal event for iguanas of all ages.

with opaque paper, cloth, or adhesive plastic may alleviate or curtail the problem.

To prevent easily startled, extremely wild specimens from repeatedly reinjuring their snouts, it may be necessary to also cover the remaining side. However, in truth this is self-defeating, for it will prevent the iguana from ever becoming accustomed to motion and your presence. Another method, one that we prefer for extremely wild specimens, is to suspend a soft cloth barrier 2 or so inches (5 cm or so) on the inside of the glass or wire sides of the cage. By coming in contact with the hanging cloth first, the iguana substantially lessens its impact with the cage side.

Toe Problems

Broken toes, torn-off toenails, and sharp claws are all frequently encountered when one works with or keeps iguanas—or, indeed, almost any other lizard.

Toes may be broken during escape efforts, or when the iguana's claws are inextricably caught in carpeting, a narrow aperture, or some other such constriction, or if the toe of a loose iguana is inadvertently stepped on. If the break is fresh and simple, the toe may often be splinted and saved. If the break is old and/or compound, amputation is usually preferred. Consult your veterinarian.

Torn-off toenails occur for the same series of reasons that breaks do. Merely apply an antiseptic oint-

If untreated, toe infections can lead to toe loss.

ment or powder and keep your iguana quiet (a towel thrown over its head will often do the trick) until the bleeding stops. These will often heal quickly without any additional procedures being necessary; however, if the toe becomes infected, consult your veterinarian.

Clipping claw tips: Iguanas of most kinds display climbing or arboreal propensities in the wild. To accommodate their climbing habits, their claws are sharp and recurved. In the wild, the normal activity pattern of the lizard usually keeps the claws somewhat dulled. Our iguanas, in their outdoor cage, merely shake their foot when I stand beside them and use the nail clipper to trim off a too-long nail. I wait a moment and clip another nail, with the same reaction. I can usually do the toes on one side with little reaction other than the foot shake. By the time the second foot has been done, the iguana has figured that I was the source of the discomfort, has tossed its head and snorted, and moved away from me.

If your iguana has to be removed from its cage for the process, the nail clipping may take a while longer. It may be a two-person job, with the iguana firmly but gently restrained and rolled onto its side with its belly facing the person who is to do the trimming. Using either human or pet nail clippers, it is then possible to carefully remove the claw tip. If the claws of baby iguanas are carefully inspected, it is often possible to see traces of venation at their cores. I peered carefully at the dark toenails of our adult iguanas and could see no vein, and at first the clipping process bothered me. Although the nails were long, I saw only minute signs of bleeding from one or two toes, and it stopped almost immediately. If you do cut a claw so short that it bleeds, apply a styptic.

Fiber constiction: Occasionally, a constriction of fiber or even unshed skin on the toe can inhibit normal blood circulation. If unresolved, this can lead to the distal portion blackening as the tissue dies, drying, and, eventually, dropping off. Normally this is not accompanied by any swelling or infection, and, in fact, is seldom detected until it is too late to correct the problem. A periodic inspection of your iguana's toes for constricting fibers or rings of dried skin, and their prompt and gentle removal if found, can lessen the probability of this occurring.

Broken Tails

Although the breaking of a tail in an otherwise perfect specimen of iguana can be disheartening, the occurrence quite probably affects the keeper more profoundly than the kept. The tails of iguanas (and most other lizards) are designed by Mother Nature to break if necessary.

Tails that are broken 50 percent or more of the way back usually regenerate more completely than those broken closer to the body. A clean, complete break will usually result in a more normally tapering, natural-appearing regenerated member. With care (and luck) a partial break may heal in a natural position. Alternatively, the break may complete itself at a later date, heal askew, or in some cases a second, abnormal-appearing tail may grow to join the first.

Tails of young iguanas broken on their distal half seldom need attention. Tails of adult iguanas broken on their distal one-third are likewise not apt to require attention. The tails of both young and old iguanas broken closer to the body may require cauterization and/or suturing to staunch blood flow and quickly close the wound.

Broken Limbs

The leg bones of an iguana are strong and designed to withstand more than considerable stress without mishap. Green iguanas have been seen to drop several dozen feet from a tree limb where they were basking to both dry ground and water. After landing on the former they scuttled off at considerable speed, showing no evidence that the drop had affected them

The regenerated tip (left) of a broken tail (center) is never as perfect as the original (right).

adversely. When landing in water they dive and swim to safety, again showing no ill effects from the considerable landing impact.

Therefore, if a captive iguana breaks its leg, it is usually the cause of either an accident or indicative of another underlying problem such as metabolic bone disease. In either case, splinting (and/or pinning, depending upon the severity and complexity of the break) will be necessary. Veterinary help should be sought immediately.

Infections

If kept clean iguanas are not likely to develop infections, even from open wounds. It is when their quarters are allowed to become dirty, or when the animals are stressed, that infections are most likely to occur. If untreated, infections can literally overwhelm even an otherwise healthy iguana in a rather short time. Abscesses, suppurations, discolorations, and other such abnormal signs may indicate either a localized or a systemic infection. A veterinarian well versed in reptilian disorders should be consulted immediately. In some cases it may be necessary to run cultures to determine an efficacious treatment. In other cases the causative agent(s) may respond quickly to broad-spectrum antibiotics. In all cases proper cleanliness of both lizard and cage are mandated.

Shedding Problems

An iguana that walks around sporting large patches of exfoliating skin is apt to be perceived as an iguana with problems. Such is not usually the case.

Reptiles shed their skin to facilitate growth. This is natural. Unlike snakes, which are well known for their entire, inverted shed skins, most lizards shed their skin less neatly and in a patchwork manner. This, too, is natural—unless the skin adheres tightly and is not lost by the lizard within a day or two. Increasing the humidity in the iguana cage and moistening your lizard's shedding skin will often help to dislodge it. A gentle tug by you on the edges may also help.

It is important, however, that you not remove the flaking skin before it is ready to be removed. The newly forming skin beneath it may be damaged if things are rushed.

Do spend a few moments checking your iguana over after each shed. Ascertain that no rings of scales remain on the digits, tail, or elsewhere, where they may then dry and restrict circulation. Should you find such problems remove them gently and promptly. It may be necessary to soak your iguana for a few minutes first to promote softening and facilitate the easy removal of the skin in question.

TIP

Salmonella, Your Iguana, and You

Iguanas, like most other reptiles and other ground-dwelling animals, such as chickens, may harbor salmonella bacteria on their skin. If you touch an iguana—or if you pick up a chicken egg or handle raw chicken—you may end up with Salmonella bacteria on your hands. Wash your hands after you handle your iguana, and don't allow children to handle your iguanas without washing their hands afterward!

GREEN IGUANA REPRODUCTION

Although many hobbyists consider merely keeping an iguana hale and hearty a sufficient challenge, there is, among iguana keepers, an ever-increasing number that wish to breed their lizards.

Why Breed Your Iguanas?

There are several reasons why keepers wish to breed their iguanas. Consider these two.

1. Probably the first is that captive breeding is a clear indication that their captive husbandry techniques work. Although the iguanas may not be behaving as they would in the wild, at least enough of the wild cues are being provided to unmask the reproductive urge.

2. Like other captive-bred reptiles, iguanas that have been born in captivity tend to be more comfortable about being around humans. Of course there's no genetic imprinting on the young that says "humans are OK," but it is very early exposure to humans, to their odors,

If you decide to try breeding iguanas, your goal is to have healthy young emerge from their eggs at the end of the incubation period.

appearance, and actions, that makes humans seem more familiar and less like enemies.

Breeding Basics

Breeding your iguanas is certainly possible, if compatible iguanas are kept in large enough facilities and are "cycled" properly. The term "cycled," as used here, pertains to the seasonal change in day length, humidity, and temperature. Day length plays a big role in evoking a breeding response, in telling their bodies that it's time to look for a receptive mate.

The breeding sequences of most reptiles and amphibians are at least partially triggered by external stimuli. Prominent among the stimuli are seasonal photoperiod, temperature, and humidity changes. Indeed, some temperate climate reptiles cannot be successfully bred unless they are subjected to a period of

CHECKLIST

What You'll Need for Breeding

1. You'll need caging large enough for courtship and an egg deposition site.

2. The lizards will probably be large enough if they are two-thirds or more grown (females, 3 feet [0.9 m] or more, and males, 4 feet [1.2 m] in length).

3. The pair needs to be compatible, as well as happy and healthy enough to breed.

4. Once bred, the female needs a deposition chamber in which to lay her clutch.

5. You need the knowledge and facilities to hatch those viable eggs that are laid. Certainly there is a ready market for those captive-bred, locally produced young.

chilling and darkness similar to what occurs during their periods of hibernation/brumation. **Note:** Brumation is the term for reptilian hibernation.

Climatic Changes

Green iguanas are tropical creatures that do not undergo extended periods of dormancy, but even in their southern haunts they experience certain annual climatic changes. For the more northerly ranging iguanas these changes include, among others, slightly reduced hours of winter daylight, slightly lowered winter nighttime temperatures, reduced winter relative humidity, and a lessening of rain activity during the winter months. The climatic changes are even less in the more tropical

areas, being largely limited to a reduction of humidity and shower activity during the winter months. Slight though these changes may be, they play a profound role in the life cycle of the green iguana. You can reproduce these changes by adhering to a natural photoperiod (turn your lights off and on with sunrise and sunset, or use a timer and increase day length with the lengthening days after the winter solstice), adding spring "rain showers," and keeping nighttime temperatures slightly lower than daytime temperatures.

In the periods of reduced light, temperature, humidity, and rainfall, hormone production is decreased. This results in ovarian and testicular regression. With the lengthening days and correspondingly increasing warmth, humidity, and rain activity of spring and summer, hormonal production again increases. Interest in reproduction picks up, and iguana-to-iguana interaction becomes a matter of territory, fighting, and sex.

Male Rivalry

Male iguanas that had previously shared the same caging arrangements will now view each other as rivals. It is at this time that what may have until then been compatible groups of iguanas are apt to become quarrelsome.

You'll need to provide some type of separation between males, because they won't remember who won the last fight; if they encounter each other, they'll fight. This sort of single-mindedness takes precedence over normal activities such as sunning or feeding, and it is stressful for both the victor and the loser, although more so for the latter.

Expect both your males and females to become less friendly toward you, and perhaps even aggressive. If one of your males stops eating in late winter or early spring, make sure that he's the only male in the cage.

Mating

If the two iguanas are male and female and relatively compatible, courtship will begin.

The courtship of a female iguana by a male is characterized by stylized body language, rather similar to that used in territoriality displays. Adult males are considerably larger than adult females. The courtship involves push-ups, head shakes, bobs and nods, and repeated dewlap distensions. The female may or may not respond by bobbing, head shakes, and push-ups; her own response is more subtle and is accomplished by her presence (she leaves if she isn't interested), and by scent. The females produce pheromones, scented "signals" that indicate willingness to breed. Males, of course, recognize these cues and respond accordingly.

Mounting: After the whirlwind courtship the male will mount the female, retaining position by grasping her nape with his jaws. The male will curve and angle his body around that of the female until cloacae are juxtapositioned. When their bodies are correctly positioned, intromission is usually quickly accomplished and is accompanied by a varied series of movements, including a "shrugging" sequence. After breeding is completed, the iguanas again go their own ways.

Nesting

From 10 to 55 eggs will be laid about 45 days later, in an area the female has carefully chosen and just as carefully prepared. After choosing a suitable site, she will dig deeply into the earth with her forefeet. Loosened dirt and debris are removed with the rear feet.

When finished, the hole will be sufficiently large for the female to completely seclude herself in while laying. Usually, several times during preparations the female will reverse her head-down position and peer quizzically from the deepening depression, perhaps scouting for approaching danger. Certainly at this time, while her head is down in a constraining hole, she is more vulnerable to predation than at almost any other time in her life.

The nesting efforts may be curtailed at any time during the preparation. If disturbed by a predator or if the digging is thwarted by a maze of roots or rocks, the female will often leave to begin anew elsewhere at another time. Even if completed after several periods of digging, interspersed with periods of rest, the female, based upon criteria known best to her, may deem the nesting chamber unsuitable. Should this be the case the female will abandon the completed but unused nest and proceed again at another location and another time.

If all is deemed well with the initial excavation, the female will, after a period of rest, lay and position each egg of her clutch then fill the hole with the removed dirt, and leave. Depending on temperature and moisture, the period of incubation can and will vary considerably. At the low end, under ideal nest conditions, the eggs may hatch in about 70 days. Under cooler, dryer conditions the incubation duration may near a full three months.

In Dade County, Florida, feral iguanas have been seen breeding (temperatures allowing) from early mid-February to late May. Nesting activities have been noted in the months of April, May, June, and July. Hatchlings have been found throughout the calendar months of summer. In that seasonally arid, almost xeric

area, females tend to construct their nests beneath moisture retaining roadside trash. Recently an egg-laden female was found during nest construction beneath a discarded damp mattress.

TIP

Breeding Iguanas

✔ To breed iguanas you will need, of course, a mature pair. Males have proportionately larger dorsal cresting, nuchal dewlap and femoral pore development, as well as a larger head and overall size.

✔ Iguanas that are tame, content, and healthy make the best breeders.

✔ If your iguanas are fearful and skittish, breeding sequences are easily interrupted.

✔ Allow your female to become accustomed to the nesting chamber, whether quasi-natural or contrived, prior to egg deposition.

A hatchling lives off of stored yolk for a day or two.

Iguanas breed somewhat earlier in their native Latin America than in Florida, and imported, captive-bred hatchlings begin flooding the pet markets in early June.

The Incubation Process

Once the eggs have been laid and the female has covered them with nesting material and departed, you need to remove the eggs and incubate them. (You may wish to wear latex gloves to keep the oils from your fingers off the eggs.) Expect to find 10 to 55 eggs (some clutches contain 80!), oval in shape with a soft, parchmentlike shell. Each egg is about 1.5 by 1 inch (38.1 × 25.4 mm).

✔ Make sure that you do not turn the eggs as you move them. If it would help, use a pencil to place an "X" on the top side of each egg before you move it, so you'll know its orientation. With reptile eggs, if the egg is "rolled over," the air pocket shifts and the embryo suffocates.

✔ Place the eggs in a series of plastic or sweater or shoe boxes that have been filled halfway with dampened vermiculite or a mixture of peat moss and potting soil. Make a depression in the surface of the vermiculite for each egg, and do not let the eggs touch each other. Cover the filled boxes and put them inside the incubator.

Chicken incubator: You can rent a chicken incubator for the period of incubation, roughly 60 to 80 days, or you can buy one from a feed store. Make certain that the one you rent or buy has a thermostat you can adjust—chicken eggs are incubated at higher temperatures than iguana eggs. You can also make your own

*Young iguanas may be barred with black
or turquoise.*

from a good-sized Styrofoam cooler, a thermo-stat/ heater, and a thermometer.

Temperature and Humidity

You'll need to monitor both the temperature and the humidity. The preferred humidity is 100 percent, which can be accomplished by keeping the hatching medium damp to the touch, but not wet. The normal temperature range for iguana egg incubation in the wild is 82 to 90°F (27.8–32.2°C), with 85 to 87°F (29.4–30.6°C) the preferred temperature.

Once you have the temperature in the incubator regulated, put the shoe/sweater boxes containing the eggs inside and close the lid. Check the temperature daily and add a little water to the medium as needed (not onto the eggs). You'll need to remove the eggs that have obvious problems, such as fuzzy mold, but since the eggs won't be touching each other, the other eggs won't be spoiled.

Knowing If the Eggs Are Fertile

How do you know if the eggs are fertile? By the end of the first week, those eggs that are *not* fertile will yellow, harden, and begin to collapse. Those that *are* fertile will remain white and turgid to the touch. Infertile eggs should be removed and thrown away.

Hatching

At then end of 60 to 80 days, plus or minus a few days on either end, if all goes well, your

*Simon Garfunkle became aggressive during
breeding season.*

baby iguanas will begin to "pip" their eggs. Iguanas in the egg bear a small egg tooth (called a caruncle) on the tip of their snout, which they use to slit the egg. The "tooth" falls off within a day or two.

The babies are really in no hurry to leave the egg. They will cut a slit, look out, and decide to stay inside the egg for a while longer, perhaps as long as a day and a half. Eventually each egg that has matured enough to hatch will do so. The live babies will emerge from the eggs and can be removed to another terrarium and offered food, water, and a sunning spot. Continue to incubate any unhatched eggs until they go bad.

Suitable Nesting Areas

Iguanas kept out-of-doors in the southernmost areas of our country can be allowed to breed and nest nearly as they would in the wild. We, as owners, merely need to ascertain that suitable nesting areas are present in the cages. In some of the more ideally arranged cages the female iguana will construct her own nest in much the way she would in the wild. If she does not initially begin her own nest, and you feel the substrate is suitable, merely disturbing the surface of the ground may be an adequate prompt.

The Outdoor Enclosure

Occasionally a female can be induced to nest naturally by providing her with a secluded area, such as the bottom third of a *large*, dark-colored plastic trash can with an entry hole cut in it, inverted over the most suitable spot, within which she may dig. In other cases, where caging conditions are less natural, a suitable nesting chamber must be constructed for the female iguana.

Several nest models seem equally well accepted by gravid female iguanas. Suitability seems governed by four considerations, these being adequate amounts of space and darkness, as well as appropriate moisture content and temperature.

An Indoor Enclosure

An "in-ground" nest can easily be made in one of two ways: by digging down and framing an adequately sized depression with wood, or by sinking the inverted bottom third of a large, dark-colored (dark brown or black), heavy plastic trash can in the ground. In either case an entryway must be left open. It will be necessary to cover the wooden chamber with a piece of plywood or other suitably opaque top. The gravid female iguana may either deposit her eggs right in this chamber as provided, or she may scratch an additional depression in the dirt that the chamber covers.

Although many breeders feel that iguanas favor rather long entranceways to their in-ground nesting chambers, they are certainly not mandatory. However, should you decide to provide one, it is

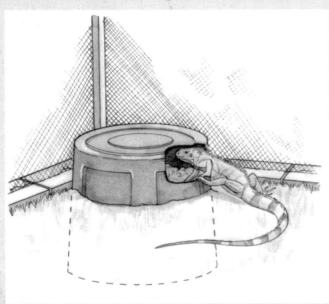

An excellent nesting chamber for an iguana may be made from the bottom third of a plastic trash can.

NESTING SITE

easily made by burying one or more lengths of ceramic pipe of suitable diameter (end to end if more than a single piece is used), sloping them from the surface to the entrance of the main nesting chamber.

The Aboveground Nest

As previously mentioned, an aboveground nest, suitable for an indoor or outdoor enclosure, can be easily made by utilizing a large, dark-colored, rigid plastic trash can. A can with four flat sides is the easiest to work with.

✔ Cut an entrance hole in an upper corner of the top.

✔ Securely affix the top to the bottom.

✔ Lay the can on one of its broad sides.

✔ Half fill the entire length of the horizontal can with a barely moistened mixture of half sand/half soil. A little peat can be mixed in to help retain moisture and lighten the mixture somewhat.

Indoor nesting chambers may be made from a rectangular plastic trash can with an entry hole cut in the lid.

✔ If the nest is to be outside, choose an area of the pen where the can will not overheat. This trash can arrangement may also be used successfully in indoor settings.

CONFESSIONS OF AN IGUANA WATCHER

Iguana watching? In the United States? Indeed, this is now possible—and, in the broader sense, when the desert iguana and chuckwallas are included under the heading, iguana watching always has been possible.

Feral Iguanas

Wild populations of the great green and two species of spiny-tailed iguanas are now firmly established in southern Florida. To observe them properly, you will need patience and binoculars. Should you choose to photograph them, you will need luck and a good telephoto lens, for feral iguanas can be as challenging to approach as the wildest bird.

Escapees from pet distributors and owners, and deliberate releases by disenchanted owners account for the majority of the iguanas now present in southern Florida. They are released in more northern climes as well, but only those released on Florida's southern peninsula, or perhaps the Lower Rio Grande Valley of Texas, are fortunate enough to find a sufficiently benign climate and adequate year-round food

A chuckwalla peers cautiously from a rocky fissure.

sources to be able to survive and establish breeding colonies. This they have done.

Reports of feral iguanas, both green and spiny-tailed, are now also common from the lower Rio Grande Valley in Texas, and spiny-tails of a different species (*Ctenosaura hemilopha* ssp.) exist in a free state on the grounds of the Arizona-Sonora Desert Museum in Tucson, Arizona.

Allow me now to transport you three quarters of the way across America to the state of Arizona, and share with you a search for our two native iguanids, the chuckwalla and the desert iguana.

The Chuckwallas

The heat from the lowering desert sun still beat mercilessly from the western sky. Spiny lizards sought respite from the unrelenting warmth in the shadows of sahuaros. The long red rays of the sun lent a touch of surrealism to the surrounding rocky ledges. We were returning to Ajo, Arizona, after a day of trying to photograph desert herps.

Our drive to Quitobaquito had been punctuated with stops and side trips to afford us more opportunity to observe herpetofauna. At many stops we had found that we were the observed long before becoming the observers. Lizards—big lizards—were watching our every move. Even before we dragged out the binoculars to ascertain their identification we instinctively knew from stance and size these lizards were chuckwallas . . . "desert chickens" or, simply, "chucks."

Habitat

Chuckwallas are inextricably associated with low, fissured ledges and boulder field habitats in the southwestern United States and Mexico. These lizards are wonderfully adapted to such habitats. They survey their domain from the summits and, when frightened, retreat (often deeply) into a fissure. If further disturbed when once in place, a chuck will inflate its body, pressing the sandpaper-textured skin tightly against the surrounding rock surfaces. This renders the lizard nearly unremovable. Although the tail of a chuckwalla will autotomize, regeneration is incomplete and often consists of little more than the healing over of the break.

Races and Species

The various races and species of chuckwallas, big, waddling, pot-bellied lizards all, are currently in taxonomic disarray. As researchers this distresses us far more than it does the lizards, who just want to be left alone to do their own things.

To keep things simple, we will continue to consider all of the stateside chuckwallas subspecies of *Sauromalus obesus*, and those from the Mexican islands as full species.

The alert lizards that we had been watching were Arizona chuckwallas, *S. o. tumidus*. This, and the westerly race, *S. o. obesus*, are the two commonly seen forms in our Southwest. The third race, the Glen Canyon chuckwalla, *S. o. multiforaminatus*, has apparently become so uncommon that it is almost never seen.

The lizards of this genus are among the few that remain in the family Iguanidae. Despite an appearance very different from that usually associated with the iguanas, the chuckwallas are a true iguana.

It is the adult males of the chucks on which maximum measurements, scale counts, and color descriptions are based. The females of most are considerably smaller than the males and usually of duller coloration.

The Sonoran chuck: Besides the three races of chuckwalla that occur north of the Mexican boundary, a Mexican endemic is recognized. This is *S. o. townsendi*, the Sonoran chuckwalla. Even adult males are of duller coloration (lacking most, if not all, of the red pigment) and marginally smaller size than the Arizona race, whose range it abuts.

The Arizona chuck: *S. o. tumidus*, the Arizona chuck, ranges from central to extreme southwestern Arizona. It also hops the border, being found in adjacent Mexico (extreme northern Sonora). It is a magnificent animal and has fewer than 50 tiny scales encircling the mid-forearm. This is a rather prominently tricolored subspecies. The head, shoulders, and forelimbs are black, the torso is brick red, the rear limbs are dark (hind feet can be light), and the tail is cream, lightest distally. A spectacular phase of this lizard occurs near Phoenix. In that area the entire head, all limbs, and torso are jet black. The tail is a brilliant fire-orange.

The western chuck: The western chuckwalla, *S. o. obesus*, a race with a tremendous range, is geographically variable in color. Found from southwestern Utah westward across Nevada to east central California, the range of this big lizard then extends southward, including all of western Arizona and the northern Baja Peninsula. At the eastern extreme of its range, the western chuckwalla is almost as brilliantly colored as the Arizona race. However, as you move westward in its range, much of the dorsal red of the lizard pales to straw yellow highlighted with black.

The Glen Canyon chuck: The Glen Canyon chuckwalla, *S. o. multiforaminatus*, has the smallest range of the four subspecies. It is found in a narrow diagonal along the Colorado River from Garfield County, Utah, to the Glen Canyon Dam in northcentral Coconino County, Arizona. The banded immatures of this race are often clad in scales of brick red. The bands, although obscuring somewhat with growth and age, are often visible throughout the life of the lizard, remaining better defined on the female.

The Peninsula chuck: The Peninsula chuckwalla, *S. (obesus) australis*, is rather similar to the western chuckwalla in appearance. The dorsal bands of this species have light centers and dark borders, thus appearing as double bands. There are more than 151 rows of ventral scales. It ranges southward in the western Baja from central Baja California Norte to the La Paz area of Baja California Sur. It appears that this subspecies has not been seen now in a number of years. Its population statistics are unknown.

The variable chuck: The variable chuckwalla, *S. varius*, is both large and attractive. Its straw-tan groundcover is overlain with variably sized and positioned patches of dark pigment. Some specimens are quite dark in overall color, but on most it is the light that prevails. Varius is found only on Isla San Esteban in the Gulf of California. The Arizona–Sonora Desert Museum in Tucson, Arizona, has researched this species extensively. Currently the museum has numerous individuals and has successfully bred and hatched the species on several occasions.

The rough-necked chuck: The rough-necked chuckwalla, *S. hispidus*, is large and nearly an overall black in coloration. The head and nape scales are enlarged and tuberculate. This is an impressive species that the Arizona–Sonora Desert Museum once worked with successfully. However, a few years ago the ASDM chose to officially discontinue the breeding project with *hispidus* and channel all efforts into their program with *S. varius*. The rough-necked chuckwalla is restricted in range to Isla Angel de la Guarda and surrounding small islands located in the Gulf of California.

S. sleveni: *S. sleveni*, a species with no common name, is restricted in distribution to Islas Carmen, Coronados, and Monserrate in the Gulf of California. Like *hispidus, sleveni* is a dark species, but is of less rugose scalation. It, like the next species, is virtually unknown in American herpetoculture.

S. ater: Like *S. sleveni, S. ater* has no common name. The latter occurs on the Gulf of California Islands of Espirutu Santo, San Francisco, Santa Cruz, San Marcos, San Diego, and Isla Partida. It is a banded species that most nearly resembles Baja's *S. australis* in both color and pattern.

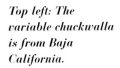

Top left: The variable chuckwalla is from Baja California.

Top right: Desert iguanas or "dipsos" feed on the leaves of the creosote bush.

Middle: The Arizona chuckwalla can be spotted in southern portions of the state for which it is named.

Bottom: This brightly colored chuckwalla morph is of very localized distribution.

The Yucatan dwarf spiny-tailed iguana only grows to about 10 inches in length.

This green iguana lives outside a restaurant in Iquitos, Peru.

Because Mexico protects all of its reptiles and amphibians and is reluctant to issue export permits to any but bona fide zoological research facilities, the Mexican species and subspecies of *Sauromalus* are very rarely encountered by herpetoculturists. However, the American *S. obesus* is still rather generally available to hobbyists.

Given low humidity, high temperatures, spacious quarters, and suitable diet, chuckwallas can and do thrive as captives. They are ideal species for advanced hobbyists and zoological institutions.

The Wild Range of Chuckwallas

✔ In the wild the range of the common chuckwalla, *S. obesus* ssp., is roughly similar to the range of the creosote bush. Besides the leaves of this desert plant, chucks consume considerable amounts of other vegetation, the flowers, leaves, and seeds of many desert annuals and perennials included. Some insects are also consumed.

✔ Chucks are oviparous lizards, the females laying a single clutch consisting of from a few to nearly a dozen large eggs. It is conjectured that many wild females produce their clutches only every second year. Captive females, traditionally better fed and having a somewhat longer annual activity period, may produce annually.

✔ Chuckwallas have a relatively short annual activity period. As would be expected from a large lizard in a temperate climate, they emerge from hibernation rather late in the year (mid- to late April, depending on temperature) and retire again well before the cold weather has truly set in. While "up and about," chucks are active only during the warmest part of the day. A body temperature of from 99 to 102°F (37.2–38.9°C) seems to be their operating optimum. At that temperature, for a big, heavy lizard, they are active, alert, wary, and even somewhat agile.

The Desert Iguana

It is from its generic name of *Dipsosaurus* that the commonly heard vernacular of "dipso" comes for this little lizard. It is also known as the "desert iguana."

Range and Species

The range of the desert iguana also follows that of the creosote bush closely and virtually parallels that of the chuckwalla. In fact, the leaves and blossoms of this desert shrub form the principal food of the desert iguana. As with the chuckwallas, controversy surrounds the exact degree of speciation of *Dipsosaurus* in general, as well as the subspeciation of *D. dorsalis*. Although some authorities feel there are as many as three species and that *dorsalis* contains three subspecies, other authorities feel that there is only the single species with no subspecies. The latter trend now seems most prevalent.

Desert iguanas are not uncommon lizards. Most are seen as a flurry of tan motions as they speed across the road. However, on each trip, we had always found the one or two specimens that hadn't safely made the dash. Even reduced to a two-dimensional road casualty from a vital desert being, the little lizards were beautiful creatures.

Desert iguanas are fairly common as far east as Arizona's Organ Pipe National Monument, but in the Dune Country of Imperial and San Diego Counties, California, we came to truly realize exactly how numerous these lizards are.

Behavior

In those areas, desert iguanas were evident everywhere. They darted along roadways, they basked in the tracery of shadows beneath leafless desert shrubs, they scurried into both isolated holes (probably of their own making, since desert iguanas are accomplished burrowers), and the entrances of kangaroo rat middens at our approach. Some even clambered about (not very gracefully, I might add) well up in the creosote bushes, stopping now and then to consume a blossom or to taste new growth. When we would approach these arboreal lizards they would "thump" heavily to the sand below and take off on a dead run toward their burrow. In those sandy, superheated, sparsely vegetated expanses, desert iguanas were abundant.

Description

The desert iguana is an attractive lizard. While heavy-bodied, it is not obesely so. It has a short head with a rounded snout, stout limbs, and a tapering tail that is about equal in length to that of the head and body. Except for the low vertebral crest the body scales are small, while those of the tail are large and arranged in prominent whorls.

While the ground color of *Dipsosaurus* varies somewhat—approximating the color of the sand in any given area—these lizards always impart the appearance of a foot-long (30-cm) tan lizard. The ground color is sandy gray and overlain on the sides with a blush of brown or brownish red. Light ocelli are present anteriorly, wavy lines posteriorly.

Given ample warmth, low humidity, brightly lit, UV-enhanced facilities, and a suitable diet, desert iguanas will thrive as captives. Some

have neared the decade and a half mark and there is little reason to believe that as we learn more about these lizards a time span of 20 years (or more) cannot be attained. Much remains to be learned about the breeding biology of these interesting aridland lizards.

Captive Care of Chuckwallas and Desert Iguanas

Providing they are given the correct caging parameters and diet, the various chuckwallas and the desert iguana do well in captivity. Lizards of both genera are captive bred in small numbers, seemingly as often by accident as purposely.

Although both of these lizards are dwellers of the deserts, chuckwallas utilize very different microhabitats than the desert iguanas. Chuckwallas are adapted to life among rocky outcrops while desert iguanas are associated with the sand, both yielding and stabilized.

Basking: Both iguanas are inveterate heliotherms—basking for long hours in the intense desert sunshine, then foraging and basking some more. When the lizards actually do near their thermal maximums, chucks retire to the comparative coolness of rock fissures or inter-boulder shadows, and desert iguanas retreat to burrows or to the tracery of shadows provided by palo verde and cresote bushes. Once cooled slightly, the lizards emerge into the sunshine to bask again. Despite being confined to desert habitats, both chuckwallas and desert iguanas are difficult to find during periods of actual drought, but are very much in evidence in years of "normal" rainfall. They are not active

In Miami, Florida, the sight of green iguanas swimming in canals is nothing unusual.

The Mexican spiny-tailed iguana may grow to 4 feet in length.

during the rains, but emerge in numbers to forage and bask on the days following.

Climbing: Despite being primarily either relatively slow-moving rock-dwellers or sand-surface speedsters, both the chuckwallas and desert iguana are fully capable of climbing and often do so—sometimes to quite considerable heights—to avail themselves of fresh leaves and succulent blossoms.

Terraria

As would be expected, captive chuckwallas and desert iguanas thrive best when given large terraria, low ambient humidity, suitable substrate, full-spectrum lighting, ample heat, and a well-rounded diet. Males are aggressive toward each other, and not more than one male of each species should be kept in a given enclosure. Providing there is sufficient space, a male will coexist well with one or more females and juveniles.

We suggest that the largest possible terrarium, but not less than 50 gallons (189 L) in size, be provided for one or a pair of either species. We prefer a 150-gallon (567-L) terrarium. This provides a floor space of 24 × 72 inches (61 × 183 cm), and allows us to provide the lizards an adequate thermal gradient and room for near-normal behavior. The basking site at the hot end of the tank is maintained at between 115 and 125°F (42.5–50.5°C). The opposite end of the terrarium is still well illuminated but cooler (80 to 90°F [26.5–31.5°C]). A natural photoperiod (daylight versus darkness) is provided. Basking sites are at the warm end of the terrarium and are illuminated and warmed with UV-A emitting bulbs in incandescent fixtures.

Substrate: For both lizard genera, the substrate is of several inches of smooth desert sand—we seldom use the sharp-silica play sand—

mixed with soil or a small amount of composted leaves. The presence of the soil or compost allows the substrate to compact well, provides a surer footing for the lizards, and, should you decide to grow live plants in the terrarium, provides these with adequate nutrition. Many desert plants, but especially the short-spined cacti, such as the many Mammillaria, are compatible with chucks and desert iguanas and help beautify any terrarium in which they are growing.

Ledges: Chuckwallas should be provided with tiered ledges that provide hiding areas along most of one long side of their terrarium. These may be of rocks or even formed of wood. If you can find it smooth enough, the pumice or lava rock sold in garden centers is lightweight, but because of the innumerable tiny pores and irregularities, it will have to be removed and sterilized regularly. Whatever you choose to use, it must be stable enough so that it will not topple and injure these heavy lizards, even during their sometimes clumsy scramblings. Yet the ledges must be able to be removed, washed, and sterilized, with a weak bleach solution or RoCal, then rinsed *very* thoroughly, whenever necessary. Chuckwallas may utilize a specific area of their terrarium, either on or off a ledge, as a defecation site. When they do this, it makes keeping the tank clean much easier than otherwise.

Outside pens: In sunbelt aridlands, or other regions with minimal rainfall and low ambient humidity, these two genera of desert iguanids may be kept in outside pens during suitable weather. If a suitable hibernaculum is provided, they may be kept outside year-round.

Breeding

Breeding occurs soon after the lizards emerge from their winter dormancy. At this time, males become agonistic, and will exact territorial dominance in many ways. Heightened colors and pattern intensities occur at this time of year. This is more apparent on desert iguanas, both sexes of which become suffused with rose on their sides, than on the darker-colored chuckwallas. During breeding season, male chuckwallas and male desert iguanas display at rival males more aggressively. If an interloper does not back down and scuttle away, actual skirmishes will occur.

Eggs: Like all other iguanids, both the chuckawalla and the desert iguana are oviparous (egg layers). It is presumed that when conditions are good, the lizards of this genera lay a single clutch a year (the desert iguana may lay two clutches), but they may forego breeding, or deposition, as well as much normal activity, in years of drought. Chuckwallas may lay as many as fifteen eggs, but more often clutches contain between four and nine eggs. Desert iguanas typically lay fewer eggs, the maximum number apparently being nine and the average five per clutch.

Deposition chambers are placed at the end of rather intricate burrows. Desert iguanas often choose to nest in the dappled sunlight beneath a desert shrub, near the roots. Chuckwallas prefer to place their clutches in burrows dug in the sand beneath or between boulders.

At deposition time, a gravid captive female will inspect her terrarium carefully, choosing an area with suitable soil temperature, and where the soil is deep, yielding enough, and containing just enough moisture to retain its structural integrity while the nest is being dug. If a suitable deposition site is not found, the female may retain her eggs so long that normal deposition is not possible. Egg solidification and dystocia (egg binding) then occurs. Should this happen, surgical removal of the eggs may be necessary to prevent the death of the female.

Incubation: At a temperature of 83 to 87°F (27.5–29.5°C), with just enough substrate moisture to prevent the eggs from desiccating, the incubation of the eggs of both species varies from about 65 to 95 days. The actual duration of the incubation is dependent upon soil temperatures and moisture content. Hatchlings vary in size, ranging from about 3 inches to just under 4 inches in total length (7.5–9.5 cm).

Diet

Although they do eat some insects (and will eat more than normal, and more than are actually good for them if given no choice) both chuckwallas and desert iguanas are primarily herbivorous lizards. High body temperatures are needed to efficiently digest the coarse vegetation that comprises the diet of wild chucks and dipsos. Because of this, these lizards are largely inactive during the late fall, winter, and early spring, with the lizards in the more northerly populations inactive for the longest duration. At the latitude of Phoenix, Arizona, chuckwallas are surface-active, temperatures allowing, from sometime in April to late September. If the weather is unseasonably warm, they may be surface-active earlier and remain so somewhat later in the year. Desert iguanas are surface-active for a somewhat longer period of time.

When captive, both chuckwallas and desert iguanas should be treated primarily as folivores. An occasional insect, blossoms, and some fruit and seeds may also be given. Such greens as mustard, collard, dandelions, nasturtium, escarole, and romaine (occasionally singly, but preferably mixed) will provide a good base diet. Chopped opuntia fruit and pads, dandelion blossoms, nasturtium blossoms, hibiscus blossoms, avocado, mango, and a bit of apple will usually be appreciated. Birdseed mixtures, dry lentils, and dry split peas will be eaten.

Additives: Calcium and vitamin D_3 additives should also be given. These additives, mixed with the food, should be provided twice weekly for fast-growing babies and ovulating females. Once weekly should be sufficient for adult males and females when not breeding. These additives are especially important when the lizards are maintained indoors and they are dependent solely on artificial lighting. High-quality, intense, UV-A/UV-B (full-spectrum) bulbs will enable these desert sun worshippers to synthesize and metabolize some percentage of their calcium needs naturally.

CHECKLIST AND COMMENTS ON THE IGUANAS OF THE WORLD

This list includes ranges, population status (when known), and zoos in which the iguanas may be seen, and special husbandry sections of the chuckwalla.

Entire populations of many species of the world's iguanas are grievously imperiled. Several species are in immediate danger of extinction, and the long-term survival of many others is seriously questioned by biologists and ecologists. Many adverse factors have been identified. These include introduced predators, introduced forage competitors, habitat degradation, and, sadly, a burgeoning illegal trade in many species. In many cases the trade is for monetary gain alone; the impetus is due to hobbyists wishing to have and/or breed an uncommon species.

Be advised that illegal dealing, either purposely or in ignorance, in endangered or threatened species—mammal, reptile, or insect—is considered a serious offense by the

The marine iguana lives in the Galapagos Islands, and eats seaweed underwater.

law enforcement arm of our Fish and Wildlife Service. The penalties can be financially devastating and may involve jail time.

The impact can be social as well: More than one dealer has had to place ads in a reptile magazine admitting his or her role in illegal animal sales.

In the following species accounts, an "(E)" preceding the name indicates a species considered endangered, "(T)" denotes a threatened species, "(NL)" denotes that the species in question is not currently listed as either threatened or endangered. The "(V)" designation for *Ctenosaura bakeri* indicates that although not listed, the species is vulnerable; "(X)" indicates a probably extinct form.

Federal permits, from the United States Fish and Wildlife Service, must be obtained before the interstate purchase and transportation, importing, or exporting of any endangered or threatened wildlife. This includes specimens otherwise legally held and captive bred. Most insular iguanas fall into this category.

Note: Most hobbyists know that common names are not well standardized. In an effort to promote uniformity, we have used names recently coined by David Blair and Robert Ehrig, well-known breeders of rare iguanas. Others are those that appear in Frank Slavens's *Reptiles and Amphibians in Captivity*. Slavens's book is also the source from which the zoo status mentioned in the following accounts has been adapted.

Species Accounts

Genus Amblyrhynchus

The single species in this genus of exclusively marine iguanas occurs on several islands in the Galapagos chain. Although not considered speciated, the iguanas among the different populations are recognizably different in appearance.

(NL) Amblyrhynchus cristatus ssp.; Galapagos Marine Iguana: (several rather poorly defined subspecies exist, each on a different island in the Galapagos Archipelago.

The adult size varies considerably, the largest specimens attaining an overall length of more than 5 feet (152 cm).

The various races of this species comprise the world's only exclusively marine lizard. They crop marine alga from rocks, diving and submerging in rather turbulent waters to do so. These lizards dine literally underwater. The short snout and powerful jaws are well adapted for such foraging, allowing the lizards ample leverage to remove these sometimes

tough simple plants from their holdtights (moorings). This species has long been protected over its entire range. The dietary necessities would make them poor candidates for successful captive husbandry even if they were not protected. Although once displayed by the Chicago Zoological Garden (Brookfield, Illinois), none have been in American collections in many years.

Genus Brachylophus

The two species in this genus are residents of Fiji and Tonga, the only true iguanas with such a distribution. These are persistently arboreal lizards. The males are strongly patterned, the females are often a unicolored green.

(E) Brachylophus fasciatus; Fiji Banded Iguana: This beautiful blue-banded green iguana (males only; females are entirely green) is classified as an endangered species; it is therefore entirely protected from harassment and exploitation. Several captive breeding programs are in place in U.S. and European zoos. This is one of a mere handful of Pacific Island iguanas. Males slightly exceed a 2½-foot (76-cm) overall length; females are somewhat smaller. Males have a low serrate crest. This species occurs on Fiji and Tonga.

This beautiful iguana may be seen in the Cincinnati, Dallas, Detroit, Fresno (California), Houston, and San Diego zoos.

(E) Brachylophus vitiensis; Fiji Crested Iguana: This species is quite similar in appearance to the Fiji banded iguana, but has a proportionately higher crest. This is especially evident in the nuchal (nape) area. The Fiji crested iguana is restricted in distribution to Fiji.

No individuals of this species are reported as being on display in zoological gardens, but a small breeding group is maintained "off display" by the San Diego Zoo.

Genus Conolophus

Of much heavier build than the marine iguana, the one or two species in this Galapagos genus are true landlubbers. In actions and diet, these land iguanas are reminiscent of the much-better-known iguanas in the West Indian genus *Cyclura*.

(E) Conolophus pallidus; Galapagos Land Iguana: Whether there is one or two species of these impressively bulky lizards will depend on the authority quoted. The land iguanas are restricted in distribution to Ecuador's Galapagos Islands and are internationally protected. Adults attain a 3½-foot (107-cm) overall length and are clad in scales of earthen tones. (This species may be identical to the next species cited.)

Reportedly, no Galapagos land iguanas of either species are in zoological collections.

(E) Conolophus subcristata; Galapagos Land Iguana: Considered by some authorities the sole species of land-dwelling iguana of the Galapagos Islands. None are displayed by zoos.

Genus Ctenosaura

The dozen or so species contained in the genus *Ctenosaura* (pronounced "ten-oh-sora") are commonly referred to as spiny-tailed iguanas. The tails of all are encircled with whorls of enlarged spiny scales that are separated from each other by one or more rows of small scales. Although these lizards are often seen on top of rock piles or on low ledges, most are well able to climb and are quite agile when in the trees. Several of the larger Mexican and Central American species, especially *C. acanthura, C.*

hemilopha, C. pectinata, and *C. similis*, are very difficult to differentiate from each other. Several of the species, *C. bakeri* and *C. oeirhina* among them, are of very restricted distribution and are poorly understood. Others are well understood and are important components of the American and European pet trades.

(NL) Ctenosaura acanthura; Spiny-tailed Iguana: This is the large spiny-tail of Mexico's Gulf Coast. It remains abundant throughout its range. Adult size is slightly in excess of 3 feet (91 cm).

Although a few of these lizards are present in private breeding collections, the only public zoological gardens reporting them is Nashville Zoo (Tennessee).

(NL) Ctenosaura bakeri; Isla Utila Spiny-tailed Iguana: Little has been published about this form which is restricted in distribution to Utila Island, Isla de Bahia, Honduras. This is now considered one of the rarest of the iguanas. Once thought extinct in the wild, *C. bakeri* was rediscovered by a research team in 1994. It was because of the unusual habitat utilized by this species—mangrove swamps—that the lizard was overlooked for so long. Other spiny-tailed iguanas inhabit sclerophyll forests and rocky deserts. It was thought in the original population estimate of *C. bakeri* that there were to be no more than a few hundred alive, and that the population consisted primarily of large males. A recovery program now in effect, and monitored by a full-time game warden, has allowed a significant increase in successful nesting and a measurable increase in juvenile examples. There is now renewed hope for the continued betterment of the population and the long-term existence of the species. No *C. bakeri* are in zoos, but a private researcher has a single male.

The Fiji banded iguana, Brachylophus fasciatus.

(NL) Ctenosaura (Enyliosaurus) clarki; Michoacan (Clark's) Dwarf Spiny-tailed Iguana: Less colorful than the closely allied Yucatan spiny-tail, Clark's spiny-tail occurs on the Pacific coast of central Mexico. This dwarfed species is adult at about one foot (30 cm) in total length. Since Mexico now protects and prohibits export, except under scientific permit, of all wildlife, *C. clarki* is seldom seen in the United States; however, Texas's Fort Worth Zoo reports having three specimens in their collection.

(NL) Ctenosaura (Enyliosaurus) defensor; Yucatan Dwarf Spiny-tailed Iguana: This is one of the smallest and most colorful of the spiny-tailed iguanas. They were once particularly common on the Yucatan Peninsula but

seem now to be reduced in numbers. This tiny iguana is primarily arboreal, darting into holes and crevices in trees when startled, and plugging the entry with its short but stoutly spined tail. Adult males attain a total length of about 10 inches (25 cm); females are smaller.

No zoological gardens have reported having this pretty little iguana on display.

(NL) Ctenosaura hemilopha conspicuosa; Mexican Spiny-tailed Iguana: This is one of the large ctenosaurs. A large, dark lizard, the Sonoran spiny-tail is widely distributed in Mexico's northern Pacific states. The tail involves more than one half of the 30-inch (76-cm) overall length.

Only the Houston Zoo (Texas) reports having this lizard on display.

The Central American dwarf spiny-tailed iguana, Ctenosaura palearis.

(NL) Ctenosaura hemilopha hemilopha; Peninsula Spiny-tailed Iguana: This is another of the large Ctenosaurs. It is abundant in eastern and southern Baja California Sur and is also found on the western mainland. Whether it occurs naturally on the Baja Peninsula, or has been introduced, is conjectural. This large iguana readily climbs the giant cacti—both alive and dead—that abound in its desert habitat. In these the lizards seek safety in woodpecker holes and other cavities. They are also abundant in rock-piles, in boulder fields, and even in urban settings.

Both the Detroit Zoo and the Arizona–Sonora Desert Museum (Tucson, Arizona) have specimens on exhibit.

(NL) Ctenosaura oeirhina; Roatan Island Spiny-tailed Iguana: This is another species with a very restricted distribution; it occurs only on Roatan Island, Honduras. Other than distribution, little is known with certainty about this species. All aspects of its life history remain enigmatic and conjectural. It is thought to be uncommon in the wild.

None are present in zoos.

(NL) Ctenosaura (Enyliosaurus) palearis; Central American (Honduran) Dwarf Spiny-tailed Iguana: This species is an inhabitant of the semiarid lowlands of Guatemala and Honduras. Large males may attain a 15-inch (43-cm) overall length. Females are smaller.

Woodland Park Zoo (Seattle, Washington) reports having this species on display.

(NL) Ctenosaura pectinata; Mexican Spiny-tailed Iguana: With adult males occasionally attaining an overall length of nearly 4 feet (122 cm), this is one of the largest of the spiny-tails. Although the natural range is from Sinaloa to Oaxaca along Mexico's Pacific Coast, newly established populations are now present in Dade and Charlotte counties, Florida, and the Lower Rio Grande Valley of Texas (Cameron and Hidalgo counties). This is an abundant species.

This species is not currently being reported in the collections of any U.S. zoo, but it is the common spiny-tail of the American pet trade, and has been established in Dade County, Florida, for at least three decades.

(NL) Ctenosaura (Enyliosaurus) quinque-carinata; Dwarf Spiny-tailed Iguana: Although this species is frequently referred to in the pet trade as the "Nicaraguan Spiny-tailed" (or "clubtailed" iguana), its actual range is from the Isthmus of Tehuantepic in Mexico's state of Oaxaca southward to Nicaragua. One of the larger of the dwarf forms, this species attains an overall length of about 17 inches (43 cm). Breeding males of this stocky little iguana assume a beautiful turquoise hue.

This species is often available in the American and European pet trades. It is reported in the collection of the Houston Zoo (Texas).

(NL) Ctenosaura similis; Spiny-tailed Iguana: With adult males nearing 4 feet (122 cm) in total length, this is one of the larger spiny-tails. It is common to abundant throughout much of southern Mexico from the northernmost areas of the Yucatan Peninsula southward to Panama. It is established in Dade County, Florida, where it may be hybridizing with *C. pectinata*, also an established species.

John Ball Zoo (Grand Rapids, Michigan); Little Rock, Arkansas; Chicago Zoological Gardens; and Dallas zoos have this species on display.

Genus Cyclura

These magnificent lizards are collectively called rock iguanas. Slender and agile when young, the adults—and especially the adult males of most species—become very heavy-bodied, some assuming almost bulldog-like proportions. Although rock iguanas can climb, most do so regularly only when juvenile. This arboreal tendency helps keep the babies away from the powerful, and potentially lethal, jaws of the adult iguanas.

Many of the rock iguanas are of West Indian distribution and are restricted to from one to a few keys (also called cays or islands). Because they are so restricted, most of the dozen or so species are of either threatened or endangered status and, until quite recently, when a specimen was found in almost impenetrable scrub by a hunting dog, the Jamaican *Cyclura collei* was thought to be extinct.

Several of the nonendangered species are occasionally seen in the pet trade.

(T) Cyclura carinata bartschi; Booby Cay (Bartschi's) Rock Iguana: In keeping with many other species of rock iguanas, males of this species are considerably larger than the females. Males may attain a snout-vent length of about 13 inches (33 cm)—total length of slightly more than 2 feet (61 cm). Females are several inches smaller. Fewer than 300 of this small rock iguana are thought to remain on its home island, Booby Cay, Bahama Islands. It is considered a threatened species; it is certainly a vulnerable species.

None are reported in the collections of public zoos.

(T) Cyclura carinata carinata; Turks and Caicos Rock Iguana: This is a slightly larger subspecies of *Cyclura carinata*. Males attain an overall length of about 15 inches (38 cm). Total length is about twice that. Females are a few inches smaller. It is thought that about 10,000 specimens remain on the Turks and Caicos Islands. Despite this not inconsiderable number, Turks and Caicos iguanas are vulnerable to both habitat degradation and human exploitation.

None are reported in zoo collections.

(E) Cyclura collei; Jamaican Rock Iguana: One of the most critically endangered of the rock iguanas, this species was thought for many years to actually be extinct. Elated researchers rediscovered the species in 1990. Although unquestionably extant, it is thought that fewer than 100 specimens survive, and these only in the remote Hellshire Hills of Jamaica. Males of this species may near, or even slightly exceed, a heavy-bodied 3½ feet (106.6 cm) in overall length. Females are somewhat smaller.

The Fort Worth Zoo (Texas) is spearheading conservation and captive breeding programs for this species. It is on display there, at the Indianapolis Zoo, and at a Jamaican research facility.

(NL) Cyclura cornuta cornuta, Hispaniolan Rhinoceros Iguana: This is not only one of the largest and most impressive of the rock iguanas, but remains one of the more common as well. Population estimates are difficult to make with any degree of accuracy on an island as large, topographically diverse, and inhospitable as Hispaniola, but there are perhaps 10,000 individuals of this big lizard left in the wild.

Because they are impressively large, inquisitive, seldom aggressive, and easily fed, this is the rock iguana most frequently seen in captivity in both private and public facilities. It is one of the few not regulated in trade in the United States by the Endangered Species Act. Captive lifespans are in excess of 25 years.

Adult male Hispaniolan rhinoceros iguanas attain massive proportions. They not only attain a total length of nearly 4 feet (122 cm), of which about half is tail, but are correspondingly heavy-bodied as well. A weight of 15 pounds (6.8 kg) is attained by some. Old males develop massive heads with greatly enlarged, rounded, temporal areas and pronounced, broadly conical nasal horns (from which both common and scientific names are derived). Although the females are smaller and less proportionately heavy, their nasal horns may be proportionately longer than those of the males.

A great many zoos have rhinoceros iguanas on display. Among other facilities, these impressive animals may be seen at the Atlanta, Bronx, Brookfield (Illinois), Dallas, El Paso, Fort Worth, Gladys Porter (Brownsville, Texas), Houston, Indianapolis, Lincoln Park (Chicago, Illinois), Louisville (Kentucky), Sedgewick County (Wichita, Kansas), Staten Island (New York), and National (Washington, D.C.) zoos.

(X) Cyclura cornuta onchioppsis; Navassa Island Rhinoceros Iguana: A somewhat smaller form of rhinoceros iguana, the Navassa Island rhino is now thought to be extinct. It was restricted in distribution to the island from which it takes its name.

(T) Cyclura cornuta stejnegeri; Mona Island Rhinoceros Iguana: As large as the nominate form, the Mona Island Rhinoceros Iguana is restricted in distribution to tiny Isla

The rhino iguana is named for the three horn nubbins on its nose.

The Mexican spiny-tailed iguana, Ctenosaura pectinata, is now established in both Florida and Texas.

Mona, east of Puerto Rico. A population of about 3,000 is estimated to remain.

Only the San Diego Zoo reports having this species in their collections.

(T) Cyclura cychlura cychlura; Andros Island Rock Iguana: This rock iguana, which attains an overall length of about 34 inches (81 cm), is restricted in distribution to Andros Island in the Bahama Islands. The females attain nearly as great a size as the males. It is possible that as many as 5,000 Andros Island rock iguanas remain in the wild.

No zoos report having the various subspecies of *C. c. cychlura* in their collections.

(T) Cyclura cychlura figginsi; Exuma Island Rock Iguana: This subspecies exists in small numbers on the central and southern Exuma

The Exuma Island rock iguana, Cyclura cychlura figginsi.

The desert iguana uses spiny bushes and rocky crevices for shelter.

Cays, Bahama Islands. It is a threatened sub-species, and probably fewer than 1,000 exist. This subspecies is smaller than the nominate form, attaining an overall length of about 30 inches (76 cm). Of this length about half is tail. It is thought that the total population of this race is less than 1,000 individuals.

(T) Cyclura cychlura inornata; Allen's Cay Rock Iguana: This 32-inch-long (81-cm) sub-species is a member of the herpetofauna of the nothern Exuma Cays, Bahamas Islands. This race is intermediate in size between the Andros and southern Exuma races. Probably fewer than 500 exist.

(T) Cyclura nubila caymanensis; Cayman Island Rock Iguana: Although originally restricted to Little Cayman Island and Cayman Brac, this race has now been introduced to Grand Cayman Island where it has been found to intergrade with the more seriously imperiled Grand Cayman blue rock iguana. A total length of slightly less than 40 inches (101.6 cm) is attained by adult males. Females are a few inches smaller. The wild population is estimated at perhaps 1,000 individuals. This rather slender rock iguana is bred in some numbers by private hobbyists and is probably second only to the rhinoceros iguana in popularity. Captive longevity of this iguana exceeds 33 years. Strangely, only private hobbyists report having this pretty iguana, but a specimen of *C. nubila* at the Atlanta Zoo is probably of this race.

(E) Cyclura nubila lewisi, Grand Cayman Blue Rock Iguana: Until recently it was esti-mated that about 250 individuals of this endangered race remained alive in the more inaccessible regions of Grand Cayman Island. However, it has recently been determined that the introduced Cayman Island rock iguana has intergraded with these slightly larger and more seriously endangered cousins. Following this revelation, DNA workups have determined that most of the blue rock iguanas in captivity in the United States were also intergrades. It is now thought that fewer than 75 pure-blooded Grand Cayman blue rock iguanas exist. Efforts are being made to maintain the pure lineage through captive breeding projects on Grand Cayman Island and at the following zoological gardens: Central Florida (Lake Monroe), Indi-anapolis, New York, Burnet Park (Syracuse, New York), and the Black Hills Reptile Garden (Rapid City, South Dakota).

(T [Cuban population], NL [Puerto Rican population]) Cyclura nubila nubila, Cuban Rock Iguana: This is both the largest and most secure of the three races of *C. nubila*. It is thought that up to 10,000 exist in the natural population on Cuba and the introduced popu-lation on Isla Mayaguez, Puerto Rico. The legal status of this animal is complicated. While the Cuban populations are considered threatened, requiring federal permits for interstate move-ment, the unprotected Puerto Rican population requires no such documentation. DNA sequenc-ing can accurately identify the origin of the specimen(s) in question. This is the largest of the rock iguanas, adult males occasionally attaining or even slightly exceeding a full 5 feet (152 cm) in length. Although smaller, the females attain a respectable 4½ feet (137 cm) in overall length.

The Indianapolis, Memphis, and Milwaukee zoos report this species in their collections.

(E) Cyclura pinguis; Anegada Island Rock Iguana: It is thought that fewer than 1,500 of these impressive 45-inch-long (114-cm) iguanas remain alive. They are restricted in distribution to Anegada Island in the British Virgin Islands. Females are somewhat smaller than the males.

None are reported in captivity.

(NL) Cyclura ricordi; Hispaniolan (or Ricord's) Rock Iguana: Only on the island of Hispaniola do two species of rock iguanas naturally coexist. This species is somewhat smaller—adult males top out at about 35 inches (89 cm)—than the sympatric rhinoceros iguana. Although an accurate estimate of the population of Ricord's rock iguana has not been possible, it is conjectured that fewer than 2,500 remain.

The Indianapolis Zoo reports having two specimens in their collection.

(T) Cyclura rileyi cristata; Sandy Cay Rock Iguana: This 24-inch (61-cm) rock iguana is restricted to a very few islands in the southern Exumas, but is not sympatric with *C. cychlura*. Perhaps as few as 250 specimens remain alive.

None of the various races of *C. rileyi* are reported captive.

(T) Cyclura rileyi nuchalis; Crooked-Acklins Island Rock Iguana: Although solidly built, even the largest males of this diminutive rock iguana seldom exceed 22 inches (51 cm) in overall length. The females are smaller. The 500 or fewer remaining specimens are restricted to cays in the Bight of Acklins, Southern Exuma Cays, and Bahamas Islands.

(E) Cyclura rileyi rileyi; San Salvador Rock Iguana: Another diminutive race, this husky little rock iguana tops out at somewhat less than a 2-foot (61-cm) overall length. It is restricted to the Cay of San Salvador in the southern Exuma Islands of the Bahamas. Estimates of the numbers remaining vary from 500 individuals to three times that number.

Genus Dipsosaurus

This small desert-dwelling iguana is native to the southwestern United States and Mexico. Primarily terrestrial, the desert iguana can climb, and ascends shrubs to procure the leaves on which its diet is based. This lizard is also a proficient burrower and is active at temperatures so high that most other lizard species have long sought the cooling shadows.

(NL) Dipsosaurus dorsalis; Desert Iguana: Whether or not subspecies exist in this foot-long (30-cm) lizard species is conjectural. The current trend, echoed here, is to consider both the genus and the species monotypic. Although some populations are suppressed by habitat degradation, in many regions this diminutive iguanid remains one of the most common of lizard species. It may be found southward from the southwestern United States (Arizona, California, Nevada, and extreme southwest Utah) southward along the entire length of Mexico's Baja Peninsula (including many islands and islets) and eastward throughout most of Sonora and northwestern Sinaloa.

A great many zoos display this little iguana. Among them are Arizona–Sonora Desert Museum (Tucson, Arizona), Honolulu, Houston, Indianapolis, John Ball Zoo (Grand Rapids, Michigan), Lincoln Park (Chicago, Illinois), Los Angeles, Louisville (Kentucky), National (Washington, D.C.), Oklahoma City, Riverside (Columbia, South Carolina), Roger Williams (Providence, Rhode Island), and Tulsa (Oklahoma).

Genus Iguana

Two easily differentiated species, one widespread and abundant, one more localized and very rare, exist. The common species is a mainstay of the pet industries of the world, and is now farmed in immense numbers in Latin

The Western chuckwalla, Sauromalus obesus obesus, *sticks close to rocky crevices when it spies humans.*

The black or rough-scaled chuckwalla, Sauromalus hispidus.

An adult male green iguana, Iguana iguana.

America for this purpose. Often quite tractable until sexual maturity is attained, reproductively active males can become suddenly savage and dangerously adversarial.

(NL) Iguana delicatissima; Antillean Green Iguana: Unfortunately, this species seems to now be losing ground because of habitat degradation and serious competition from the introduced common green iguana. The historic range included many of the islands of the Lesser Antilles. This species nears 5.5 feet (165 cm) in length. Females and young are green in the wild, but when kept captive soon become gray. Males are duller, but when breeding develop a pink to rose suffusion on their jowls. This species has proven difficult as a captive, and although fertile eggs have now been produced by captive females, successful hatching has not yet occurred.

Only the Memphis and the San Diego zoos report this increasingly rare iguana in their collections.

(NL) Iguana iguana; Giant Green Iguana: This is the most widely ranging iguanid. It occurs naturally from northern Mexico to southern Brazil and westward to Paraguay, and on some islands of the Lesser Antilles; it has been introduced and established on others, and is also present in breeding colonies in Florida and Hawaii. It is also established in Cameron County, Texas, in the Lower Rio Grande Valley. Adult males occasionally exceed 6 feet (183 cm) in length.

This species is present in nearly every zoological garden and in thousands of private homes and pet shops throughout the world.

Genus Sauromalus

This genus of several species is currently in taxonomic disarray. Some species are endangered. The more common species are adult at about 16 inches (40.6 cm) in overall length. Some of the rarer types near 2 feet (61 cm) long. One species is widespread in the deserts of the American Southwest and in Mexico. Several species are restricted to small islands in the Sea of Cortez. Most are clad in the hues of the sands and rocks on which they dwell. Females are often smaller than the males and are of a duller color.

(NL) Sauromalus ater ater, Chuckwalla: This species is restricted in distribution to the Mexican Islands of Espiritu Santo, San Francisco, San Jose, Santa Cruz, San Diego, and Isla Partida in the Gulf of California. Large males attain more than 16 inches (40.6 cm). Females are smaller.

No zoological facilities have listed any race of this species in their present collections.

(NL) Sauromalus ater klauberi, Chuckwalla: This race is known only from Santa Catalina Island in the Gulf of California.

(NL) Sauromalus ater shawi, Chuckwalla: This Mexican rarity is restricted to Isla San Marcos in Mexico's Gulf of California.

(NL) Sauromalus australis, Baja Peninsula Chuckwalla: This species is found in southeastern Baja California Norte and most of eastern Baja California Sur, south to La Paz. Considered a subspecies of *S. obesus* by some authorities, momentum to consider the animal a full species is now picking up. Adult males may occasionally exceed 16 inches (40.6 cm). Females are smaller.

There are apparently no Baja Peninsula chuckwallas captive in public collections.

(NL) Sauromalus hispidus, Black (Rough-Scaled) Chuckwalla: This is another insular form from Mexico's Gulf of California. It occurs only on the island of Angel de la Guarda and its surrounding satellites. This species nears 2 feet (61 cm) in length. The neck scales are protuberant and roughened.

Currently this species is reported in the collection of only the Arizona–Sonora Desert Museum (Tucson, Arizona).

(NL) Sauromalus obesus multiforaminatus, Glen Canyon Chuckwalla: This subspecies occurs in a narrow diagonal along the Colorado River from Garfield County, Utah, to the Glen Canyon Dam in northcentral Coconino County, Arizona. It has apparently not been seen in several years and the population statistics are unknown. Large males may exceed 16 inches (40.6 cm). Females are smaller.

It is not reported in the collection of any zoo.

(NL) Sauromalus obesus obesus, Western Chuckwalla: This widespread and rather common lizard is found in suitable rocky habitats from southwestern Utah westward across Nevada to east central California, then southward through all of western Arizona and the northern Baja Peninsula. It is in the collection of dozens of zoos, and in the United States has been bred in many zoological facilities.

(NL) Sauromalus obesus townsendi, Sonoran Desert Chuckwalla: This race is found only in the western sections of the Mexican State of Sonora and on a very few of the islands that lie just off the coast in the eastern Gulf of California. It is not known to be in any zoological collection.

(NL) Sauromalus obesus tumidus; Arizona Chuckwalla: This is the chuckwalla seen in central and extreme southwestern Arizona and southwestern Sonora, Mexico. It is attractive and abundant in suitably rocky habitats. It is reported in the collections of the Arizona–Sonora Desert Museum (Tucson, Arizona) and the Riverbanks Zoological Park (Columbia, South Carolina).

(NL) Sauromalus sleveni; Chuckwalla: Another on the western Gulf of California insular forms, *S. sleveni* is restricted in distribution to Islas Carmen, Coronados, and Monserrate. It is seldom seen. Adult males near a foot and a half (45.7 cm) in length.

No public facility has listed this species in their collections.

(E) Sauromalus varius; San Esteban (Painted) Chuckwalla: The largest of the chuckwallas, *S. varius,* occasionally attains a 2-foot (61-cm) overall length. It is restricted in distribution to Mexico's Islas San Esteban, Lobos, and Pelicano in the western Gulf of California.

More than a dozen facilities are working with this impressive chuckwalla. Among others are the Arizona–Sonora Desert Museum (Tucson, Arizona), Houston Zoo, Louisville Zoo (Kentucky), and the Rio Grande Zoo (Albuquerque, New Mexico).

Opposite page top: The peninsula spiny-tailed iguana, Ctenosaura hemilopha hemilopha.

Opposite page bottom: The Cayman Island rock iguana, Cyclura nubila caymanensis.

Top: The Allen's Cay rock iguana, Cyclura cychlura inornata, *is a striking lizard. Unfortunately it is quite rare at the present time.*

Bottom: The dwarf spiny-tailed iguana, Ctenosaura quinquecarinata.

Glossary

Aestivation a period of warm weather inactivity, the summertime equivalent of hibernation

Allopatric not occurring together but often adjacent

Ambient temperature the temperature of the environment

Anterior toward the front

Arboreal tree-dwelling

Attenuated long and slender, as an iguana's original tail

Autotomize the ability to break easily or voluntarily cast off a part of the body.

Brumation the reptilian and amphibian equivalent of mammalian hibernation

Caudal pertaining to the tail

Cloaca the common chamber into which digestive, urinary, and reproductive systems empty and that opens exteriorly through the vent or anus

Crepuscular active at dusk or dawn

Crest a ridge, usually of enlarged or attenuated scales along the nape, back, and/or basal tail area of an iguana

Deposition the laying of eggs

Deposition site spot chosen by the female to lay eggs.

Dichromatic two color phases of the same species

Dimorphic a difference in form, build, or coloration involving the same species

Diurnal active in the daytime

Dorsal pertaining to the back; upper surface

Dorsum the upper surface

Endemic confined to a specific region

Femoral pores openings on the underside of the thighs of lizards; they produce a waxy exudate

Femur the part of the leg between hip and knee

Form an identifiable species or subspecies

Fracture planes softer areas in the tail vertebrae that allow the tail to break easily

Genus a group of species having similar characteristics

Granular pertaining to small, flat scales

Gravid the reptilian equivalent of mammalian pregnancy

Gular pertaining to the throat

Heliothermic pertaining to a species that basks in the sun

Hemipenes the dual copulatory organs of male lizards and snakes

Hybrid offspring resulting from the breeding of two species

Insular island-dwelling

Intergrade offspring of the breeding of two subspecies

Juvenile a young or immature specimen

Keel a ridge (along the center of a scale)

Labial pertaining to the lips

Lateral pertaining to the side

Melanism a profusion of black pigment

Middorsal pertaining to the middle of the back

Midventral pertaining to the center of the abdomen

Monotypic having but one type

Nocturnal active at night

Ocelli dots or "eye spots" (often with a light-colored center) on a lizard's skin

Oviparous reproducing with eggs that hatch after laying

Ovoviviparous reproducing with shelled or membrane-contained eggs that hatch prior to, or at, deposition

Parietal eye a sensory organ positioned mid-cranially in certain reptiles

Phalanges bones of the toes

Poikilothermic a species with no internal body temperature regulation; "cold-blooded"

Race a subspecies

Rugose not smooth; wrinkled or tuberculate

Saxicolous rock-dwelling

Serrate sawlike

Species a group of similar creatures that produce viable young when breeding.

Subspecies the subdivision of a species; a race that may differ slightly in color, size, scalation, or other criteria

Sympatric occurring together

Taxonomy the classification of plants and animals

Terrestrial land-dwelling

Thermoregulate to regulate (body) temperature by choosing a warmer or cooler environment

Thigmothermic pertaining to a species (often nocturnal) that thermoregulates by being in contact with a preheated surface, such as a boulder

Tubercles warty protuberances

Tympanum the external eardrum

Vent the external opening of the cloaca; the anus

Venter the belly

Ventral pertaining to the undersurface or belly

Herpetological Societies

Reptile and amphibian special-interest groups exist in the form of clubs, monthly magazines, and professional societies, in addition to herp expos and other commercial functions mentioned elsewhere.

Herpetological societies (or clubs) exist in major cities in North America, Europe, and other areas of the world. Most have monthly meetings; some publish newsletters, many host or sponsor field trips, picnics, or other interactive functions. Among the members are enthusiasts of varying ages and levels of expertise. Information about these clubs can often be learned by querying pet shop employees, high school science teachers, university biology department professors, or curators or employees at the department of herpetology at local museums and zoos. All such clubs welcome inquiries and new members.

Two of the professional herpetological societies with publications are:

Society for the Study of Amphibians
    and Reptiles (SSAR)
St. Louis University
3507 Laclede
St. Louis, Missouri 63103

Herpetologist's League
Division of Biological Sciences
Emporia State University
Emporia, Kansas 66801

Publications

The SSAR publishes two quarterly journals: *Herpetological Review* contains husbandry, range extensions, news on ongoing field studies, and so on; the *Journal of Herpetology* contains articles more oriented toward academic herpetology.

Reptiles Magazine publishes articles on all aspects of herpetology and herpetoculture (including iguanas). This monthly also carries classified ads and news about herp expos. Their address is *Reptiles Magazine,* P.O. Box 6050, Mission Viejo, California 92690.

Internet

One of the most popular Internet addresses is *www.kingsnake.com.*

This site provides an immensely active classified section, interactive forums, periodic chats, and web-radio interviews. Because of the ability to post and view photos of iguanas being offered for sale, this site should be of great interest to all hobbyists.

The International Iguana Society

The International Iguana Society (Route 3, Box 328, Big Pine Key, Florida 33043) is a nonprofit corporation dedicated to the conservation, biological diversity, and the herpetoculture of the iguanas of the world. Recognizing that many taxa are in immediate jeopardy, the IIS is attempting to help the appropriate governments and governmental agencies establish guidelines

A bookcase is a favorite hiding place for an escaped iguana.

to assure the continued existence of all iguanid lizards. Although the main thrust of the IIS is oriented toward the various West Indian rock iguanas of the genus *Cyclura*, problems concerning all iguanid taxa are recognized and considered. A quarterly newsletter, the "Iguana Times," is sent to members.

Iguana Rescue Societies

With the almost exponential proliferation of great green iguanas in the pet trade, it was only reasonable to expect that many of the owners who purchased on impulse an 8-inch-long (20-cm) baby that was only as big around as your little finger were ill-prepared to care for the lizard as it grew. The problem could be likened to having room and resources for a Chihuahua but then acquiring a St. Bernard puppy simply because it was there and cute.

Baby iguanas are not difficult to care for, and they are easy to love. Considering the space factor alone, that cannot be said for the adults of the species. Faced suddenly with the seemingly insurmountable problem of having far too much lizard for far too little space, green iguanas are often unceremoniously disposed of. Sadly, some are merely taken to the nearest city park and quietly turned loose. In areas such as Brownsville, Texas, and Miami, Florida, the lizards often thrive and become part of a feral iguana community (be advised that it is illegal to turn an exotic animal loose). North of those two cities the low temperatures associated with a normal winter are quickly fatal to the lizards. Unwanted adult iguanas are not easy to place in foster facilities. Humane societies often will not accept the lizards.

To help you understand the magnitude of the problem, simply scan some of the queries placed at the site of Iguana Adoption/Rescue Information. Their web address is *http://www.geocities. com/Heartland/6860/ig-adopt.html.*

Another site of interest is that of National Iguana Awareness Day. Their web address is *http://www.niad.org/International/index.html.*

Dozens of iguana rescue sites have sprung up in recent years. Almost all of these are private

Acknowledgments
Thanks are due to Mike Beaver, Mike Ellard, Bill Griswold, D.V.M., Bill Love, Rob MacInnes, Chris McQuade, and Sheila Rodgers for providing photographic opportunities.

Ellen and Bob Nicol shared with us some observations on their own iguanas—lizards that, we are sure, consider themselves people.

Food values were excerpted from charts first made public by the long-defunct International Turtle and Tortoise Society.

We wish to extend special acknowledgment to some individuals for their published contributions on the captive care of green iguanas: Philippe DeVosjoli, Bob Ehrig, James Hatfield, Fredric L. Frye, D.V.M., Florence Gutierrez, D.V.M., and Terry Reed. Dr. Frye also read the manuscript and provided comments and suggestions that have helped us improve the quality of our presentation.

organizations, and most are struggling financially. To view just a few of the organizations, have your search engine scan "Iguana Rescue." Other rescue societies may be listed in your local phone book, or be known to pet store owners, biology teachers, or museum staff. Inquire, but please, choose an equable solution not only for you but for your lizard as well. Always remember that your iguana is an unwitting and unwilling component of the pet trade that is deserving of the utmost respect from its owner.

INDEX

About the Authors

R. D. Bartlett is a herpetologist who has authored more than 350 articles and three books on reptiles. He lectures extensively and has participated in field studies across North and Latin America.

In 1978 he began the Reptilian Breeding and Research Institute (RBRI), a private facility. Since its inception, more than 150 species of reptiles and amphibians have been bred at RBRI, some for the first time in the United States under captive conditions. Successes at the RBRI include several endangered species.

Bartlett is a member of numerous herpetological and conservation organizations.

Patricia Bartlett received her degree from Colorado State University. She has worked in publishing and museums.

Photo Credits

Mella Panzella: page 61; R. D. Bartlett: pages 2-3, 4, 8 top, 12, 13, 16 left and right, 17 left and right, 20, 24, 25, 28 left and right, 29 top right, bottom, 33, 36 top, 37 left and right, 40, 41, 44, 45, 48, 49, 52, 53, 56, 57 top, 60, 64 all photos, 65 top and bottom, 68, 69, 72, 73, 76, 77, 80 top and bottom, 81 top and bottom, 84 top and bottom, 85, 88 top and bottom, 89 top and bottom, 92; Zig Leszczynski: pages 5, 9 top left and right, 21, 29 top left, 32, 36 center and bottom; Joan Balzarini: 8 bottom, 9 bottom, 57 bottom.

Cover Photos

All covers by R. D. Bartlett.

Important Note

Before using any of the electrical equipment described in this book, be sure to read Avoiding Electrical Accidents on page 18.

While handling iguanas you may occasionally receive bites, scratches, or tail blows. If your skin is broken, see your physician immediately.

Some terrarium plants may be harmful to the skin or mucous membranes of human beings. If you notice any signs of irritation, wash the area thoroughly. See your physician if the condition persists.

Iguanas may transmit certain infections to humans. Always wash your hands carefully after handling your specimens. Always supervise children who wish to observe your iguanas.

All inquiries should be addressed to:
Barron's Educational Series, Inc.
250 Wireless Boulevard
Hauppauge, NY 11788
http://www.barronseduc.com

International Standard Book No. 0-7641-1993-1

Library of Congress Catalog Card No. 2002018674

Library of Congress Cataloging-in-Publication Data
Bartlett, Richard D., 1938–
    Iguanas : everything about selection, care, nutrition, diseases, breeding, and behavior / R.D. Bartlett and Patricia P. Bartlett ; illustrations by Michele Earle-Bridges.
        p. cm.
    Includes bibliographical references (p.).
    ISBN 0-7641-1993-1
    1. Iguanas as pets. I. Bartlett, Patricia Pope, 1949– . II. Earle-Bridges, Michele. III. Title.

SF459.I38 B37 2003
639.3'9542—dc21   2002018674

Printed in Hong Kong
9 8 7 6 5 4 3 2 1